The Boy from Block 66

Moshe Kessler dedicates this book with everlasting love and longing to the memory of his beloved family:

Mother - Paula Pearl, daughter of Zeev Blaubstein

Father - Herman Zvi Ben Meir HaCohen Kessler

Brother - Arnold Chaim Leib Ben Zvi Kessler

The Boy from
Block 66

Limor Regev

The Children Saved from the Death March
by the Buchenwald Camp Resistance

The authorised biography of Moshe Kessler

First published in 2023 by eBookPro
www.ebook-pro.com

First published in the UK in 2024 by Ad Lib Publishers Ltd
15 Church Road
London, SW13 9HE
www.adlibpublishers.com

Paperback ISBN 9781802472509

A CIP catalogue record for this book is available from the British Library.

Every reasonable effort has been made to trace copyright-holders of material reproduced in this book, but if any have been inadvertently overlooked the publishers would be glad to hear from them.

Printed in the UK

10 9 8 7 6 5 4 3 2 1

הכרת תודה ומסירות

לזכר חוותי רבקה בת-שבע ושמואל והמשפחה ספרי רב

אונו, ובזה הזכרון הזה אל ההורים. לפני כמה שנים
סיפרה אנושי לגלות ל בהם מעניין הסיפור שלה
ואיכה אם עם אתה הזמן מעניין לאוך תולדה זו בשם
הסיפור זה זו, ומנגמה הזה מסתורין.

ראבר ליכן אחד הסיפור מאתים אם הראשונה ב תגבד פעם אל
מזה ... בתגלות, ... לנ... והמשפחה הזו הרן האחותיות.
כאשר אתם ... לאור את הדרא... את הספר.

נתונים ... הסיפורים שלנו כ ... מתארו ... לקחת חלק
ב הסיפור ... של חוית ליהוי ... לגלות היאא
... ותחתך השואות ואובדות ... הוא הם ... לנוף האאות
ל הינת תודות, ... לני ... ... 1949.
ה ... שנה - 2020 ... מתוין את חוית ... ...
... הראשונים רבה אל ... הישרא ... פה אינה
אל הם ... אומר ל חוות אל קיצלה , מ ... ב.

In Gratitude –

To Dr. Limor Regev, the initiator and author of this book

Limor is a friend of my daughter, Anat Himmelhoch. A few years ago, she expressed to Anat her interest in personal Holocaust histories. She asked Anat if there would be an interest and willingness for me to tell my story. Anat was uncertain.

Some months later, Limor and her family were among the invited guests at the Bar Mitzvah of my youngest grandson Roei Himmelhoch,

Subsequently, she once again raised the issue. At my advanced age, I felt it my responsibility to preserve my personal story for my family and for future generations.

I began meeting weekly with Limor, during which my life story began unfolding with Limor's encouragement.

It began with stories of my childhood and led up to my Aliyah to Israel in January 1949.

As a result, at the start of 2021, Limor presented me with the story in print. I read it with great excitement, pleased and gratified by her beautiful literary style.

I offer you my sincere and heartfelt thanks, Limor.

Moshe

Contents

"Roy's grandfather Moshe, please come up for the blessing."

I rose and slowly straightened up. With small steps, I walked towards my grandson, who stood before me in a white dress shirt, happy and excited. I smiled at him. The little blond boy who used to run to me every Monday on the path from his kindergarten, jumping up high, and putting his little hand in mine so I could walk him home had become a tall and handsome young man. I paused and gazed round at the dozens of relatives and friends who were there to celebrate his Bar Mitzvah. They sat at tables laden with all good things.

Tears welled up in my eyes. I took a deep breath and tightened my grip on the ancient prayer book that belonged to the family of Eva, my wife. The books had been kept in an out-of-the-way private prayer room in Slovakia, safe from harm and were brought to Israel by Eva's family. At the Bar Mitzvahs of each of my grandchildren, we passed them on for future generations. In my other hand, I held a white yarmulke. When I put it on Roy's head and saw his blue eyes looking at me, the memories flooded over me once again.

Just as I did two years earlier at Itai's Bar Mitzvah celebration, I closed my eyes and struggled to drive out of my mind the images that flashed in front of my eyes. They were as real and alive as if they had happened only yesterday, and not decades ago. I opened my eyes again. Roy looked at me with a worried expression on his face. I smiled at him, letting his gaze of concern help me come back to the present. I handed him the prayer book and he held it tightly. Tears of excitement and pride welled up in my throat at the sight of my grandson holding in his hands a permanent legacy of the lost families and the world of my childhood.

I spent the rest of the evening pleasantly talking and laughing with our relatives and friends.

That night I had a hard time falling asleep. My thoughts wandered back to many years earlier, to that innocent child who impatiently waited for the moment when he would celebrate his entry into the adult world. I was eager to celebrate my bar mitzvah in the beautiful Great Synagogue of Berehovo, the Czech town where I was born and raised. The Great Synagogue was always crowded on Saturdays and holidays and I remember well its atmosphere of holiness.

When I was a small child and we used to come to family and friends' events held in the synagogue, I always thought about the moment when my big day would come. I would imagine myself standing there in festive attire, reading in a clear voice from the Sefer Torah with my father by my side, wrapped in a festive tallit, his hand on my shoulder. In the congregation, I would picture my grandfather leaning over the prayer book on his regular davening bench, completely enveloped in his white prayer shawl, and looking up at us proudly from time to time. I could see in my mind's eye my little brother next to him and my mother peering at us excitedly from the women's section. The synagogue would be filled to overflowing to accommodate our entire extended family, my school friends, and our many acquaintances in the community.

The reality was different from anything I had imagined. The synagogue was not only not crowded; it was empty, except for a few older men and women. By this time only the elderly, women and children remained in our community. All the others had been drafted, among them my father and all the other men aged twenty and above, including a great many of our acquaintances and family members. Grandpa had passed away a long time before and there was no male relative with me on the momentous occasion. I delivered my sermon with only my mother's sad eyes gazing from the women's section. The atmosphere in the synagogue was gloomy and oppressive, and sorrow permeated the air. It was a scene very different from what I had always imagined. It was two days before Rosh Hashanah, September 27, 1943.

Let me start from the beginning…

A Happy Childhood

Berehovo 1930-1939

I was born in Czechoslovakia, in an area called Carpathia-Russia. It was located near Czechoslovakia's border with Hungary, Romania and Poland, so there was a diverse population of different ethnic groups who spoke many languages. It is a little hard to believe, but in less than thirty years our city was part of four different countries and its name was changed several times. The two world wars brought about these changes and they left a distinct mark on where we lived. The changes also had a significant and profound effect on the fate of the Jews of my city.

Until the end of World War I in 1919, the entire area of Carpatho-Russia had been part of the vast Austro-Hungarian Empire. Before I was born, our town was Hungarian, and was called Burgsass. The inhabitants considered themselves Hungarians to all intents and purposes. The dominant language in the streets of my hometown was Hungarian, as was the culture and national character. The end of the First World War brought about many changes, and the countries that lost the war had to pay in territory which was taken from them and transferred to emerging nation-states established after the war. The Austro-Hungarian Empire collapsed and within its enormous territories were Poland, Yugoslavia, Czechoslovakia and the modern Hungarian state.

Germany, the biggest loser in the war, forfeited many territories, among them the Sudetenland, which was annexed to Czechoslovakia. Hungary, an ally of Germany. was forced to give up the entire Carpatho-Russia region. This also became part of the new state of Czechoslovakia. Therefore, the new country was established on some land that had been part of Germany and some that had belonged to Hungary until 1918. Germany found it difficult to accept the separation from the Sudetenland, where three million ethnic Germans lived.

The newly established Hungarian state was frustrated by the transfer of Carpatho-Russia and the forced farewell to the dream of a "Greater Hungary." These two issues will be an important key to understanding the events that will take place twenty years later in 1938, ushering in the opening events of World War II.

In the meantime, in 1919 the inhabitants of our area changed from Hungarian citizens of The Austro-Hungarian Empire to citizens of the new state of Czechoslovakia. The name of our city also changed. It was now Berehovo, and not Burgsass. However, when territory changes hands and flies a different flag, it does not necessarily mean that civilians in the area experience a similar change. People's emotional attachments do not change rapidly and they do not adapt to match the pace of political or international upheaval. Even under the Czech flag, many of the inhabitants of our region continued speaking Hungarian and preserved Hungarian traditions and customs, which had been part of their lives for centuries.

For most of the population, the change was artificial and did not match their national feeling and pride. They remained loyal to their Hungarian identity.

This fact has had a profound effect on our lives.

My father, Herman Zvi Kessler in the uniform
of the Czech army

This all happened before I was born, but the historical background is very important to understand the sequence of events.

In most of the homes in Berehovo, Hungarian was spoken in addition to Czech, which was the official language. Most of the schools were Czech but there were also Hungarian educational institutions. We Jews also spoke Yiddish and in fact, from a young age I spoke three languages on a daily and regular basis.

We were happy to be part of the Czechoslovakia. The young state had instituted equal opportunities and enabled many of us to improve our economic situation through hard work and education. Our gentile friends and neighbors did not take advantage of this opportunity. Beneath the surface, many of them resented the progress made by the Jews in the Czech state while many of our neighbors remained loyal Hungarians.

Berehovo was a typical country town, encircled by rustic hillsides, villages, and agricultural areas. We could see the many wineries surrounding us from the city streets. The Horca River flowed through the city, and its beating heart was the wide main street called the Corso, the promenade.

The Jews in Berehovo controlled trade and the liberal professions; they set up factories and purchased estates and vineyards.

Jews set up large factories in Berehovo, including the brick factories and the lumberyards, coalmines and flourmills. Others owned many of the shops in the markets, as well as the pharmacies and a large hotel on Main Street. Our gentile neighbors were envious of our success. They had the same initial opportunity but were unable to take advantage of it. Our Jewish community encouraged education along with hard work. To make a living, we worked diligently and did not go to the taverns. Due to perseverance and hard work, many of our people's businesses flourished, and thanks to our education we stood out in the liberal professions. The great majority of the doctors, lawyers, and engineers in Berehovo were Jewish.

Berehovo was a relatively small town and we Jews made up about a third of the population. Almost everyone knew each other and we felt safe walking the streets, many of which had Jewish businesses. Our community was prominent in higher educational institutions as well.

In these successes lay the seeds of hostility and jealousy that would appear later. The Gentiles witnessed the growing number of large Jewish landowners and successful Jewish businesses, compared to the mass of simple workers who lived in poverty and found it difficult to support their families. Gradually, hostility grew in their hearts in light of the economic boom and the Jewish strength in industry and commerce.

We Jews were not at all aware of the feelings that bubbled beneath the surface among our non-Jewish friends and neighbors that would erupt and release fiery volcanic lava when the groundwork was ready for it.

Education and solid economic status did not mean we gave up religious symbols. We strictly preserved the Jewish traditions. Some of us defined ourselves as ultra-Orthodox and dressed accordingly, but we were all traditionalists and we were very stringent about keeping the religious commandments. Jewish men wore hats to cover their heads and we children did the same. Our clothes were normal everyday wear. My father wore a hat, but did not grow a beard.

A hat was actually the yarmulke of those days - the hallmark of our parents as wells as ours, their children.

Like all the Jewish families in Berehovo, we observed the Shabbat and the kosher laws. We went to synagogue regularly and observed all the holidays.

Religion was an integral part of our daily lives. The young Czech state supported religious freedom, so we did not feel cut off or threatened in any way.

Our community was well known in the surrounding region for the many active prayer and Torah institutions, which were scattered throughout it. The great synagogue of Berehovo stood in all its glory in the city center, and was a magnet on Saturdays and holidays. Additional houses of worship, ritual baths, religious schools and other small educational institutions were all throughout the city. We made sure to observe the religious laws. It was a tradition passed down from generation to generation.

On Yom Kippur we would flock to the synagogue. A holiday atmosphere filled the city streets and in the public spaces people would greet each other with 'May you be written in the Book of Life.' Due to the substantial presence of the Jews in the cultural life of the city and the commitment to the mitzvah of 'man and his friend,' Yom Kippur left its mark on the entire city.

Every Friday before dinner Dad, my little brother Arnold and I would go to the neighborhood synagogue which was near where we lived. After the services, we would return home, recite the blessing over the wine, and enjoy my mother's delicacies. I loved Friday night dinner in my parents' house. After eating, we would see grandpa, grandma and our uncles and aunts. We would sit together and talk amongst ourselves until the late hours of the evening.

On Saturday mornings we would go to the more central synagogue, "Oseh Hesed" ("Doing kindness"). It was the second largest synagogue in Berehovo, only slightly smaller than the magnificent synagogue in the city center. It was about a twenty-five minute walk from our house. On the holidays we would all walk to the synagogue, dressed in white. On every street corner we would meet neighbors and acquaintances.

Relatives, who visited the town after the war, said that a monument had been erected in the courtyard of the "Doing Kindness" synagogue, which still exists today, commemorating the thousands of victims: the city's Jews.

We spent most of Saturday at home with the family. The streets were quiet. Most households did not have private cars at that time and the main public transport was by carriage, driven by a coachman. We traveled very little, even on weekdays. Our main means of getting around was on foot.

Every Saturday afternoon we would walk the streets of the city. I remember the young people, sitting on benches spread along the main street, in the tree-lined boulevards. Crowds of young people would crowd the area, talking and laughing.

We defined ourselves as religious-Zionist. Unlike many countries of Western Europe where Jews distanced themselves from Judaism and adhered to secular Zionism, – my parents saw religion as an integral part of their being Zionists and they kept the traditions and observances.

Berehovo had a large Zionist organization and my father was an active participant. In my early childhood, my family was offered a certificate of immigration to Eretz Israel. In those years, it was still possible to immigrate to Israel, and after the Nazis came to power in Germany in 1933, many Jews decided to leave Europe and immigrate to Israel. During this period, anti-Semitism increased in Nazi Germany and in Eastern European countries, but where we lived there was no feeling of hostility from our surroundings or fear among the Jews. Anti-Semitism was not something we knew, as children.

My parents debated leaving. My father, who was an ardent Zionist, wanted very much to go to Eretz Israel, but my parents consulted with members of the extended family, and they all expressed reservations in principle about the idea. There was no possibility that all the family members could come, as the number of permits was limited. Even if it were possible,- I am not sure that in those days, when Jews in our area felt no danger, that my family would all decide to leave a place that had been their home for generations.

The members of our extended family were unanimous, because if the whole family remained in Czechoslovakia, my father and mother's move to a distant, isolated place would result in their feeling a sense of loneliness. Family relationships in the Jewish community were warm, very close, and full of mutual caring. Our lives were pleasant and good, filled with many moments of joy and celebration in the company of our extended family, who all lived in the city.

Besides, the Land of Israel was known to have a hot and steamy climate, and was undeveloped in terms of infrastructure or places of employment and was under the full control of Great Britain. It was not clear how they could make a living, and the change sounded particularly challenging.

The idea was shelved.

I had a very happy childhood in Berehovo.

We lived at 46 Seicheni Street, a quiet side street. It was close to the city center, with a spacious compound that included a store for groceries and household times. There were also residential buildings, and other properties.

Our living area included three apartments with spacious rooms. My grandparents, Clara and Meir Kessler, lived in one apartment. My uncle and aunt, Shloima (Shlomo) and Hani Leinsider and their two children Magda and Zulik lived in the second apartment, and the last apartment was our home, where my parents Herman and Paula Kessler lived with my brother Arnold and me.

Grandma and Grandpa Kessler before the war

My uncle Shlomo Laisinder

Aunt Hani was my father's sister and they were very close. Arnold and I were also very close to our two cousins, Magda and Zulik and we would spend our best times together.

Mother, Father, Arnold and me. Dad's furlough, 1943

At the entrance to our living complex was a large, beautiful pecan tree, whose wide branches we could see from our dining room window. We kids waited every year for when the pecans would ripen and we spent hours climbing the tree branches to pick them and collect the fallen nuts. The pecan nut grows wrapped in a green peel and when we took it off to gobble up the pecans, we got brown stains on our hands. Our parents used to scold us because the stains were stubborn and hard to remove. All through my childhood the pecan tree was with me and it is etched in my memory to this day.

A wide wooden door led from the compound entrance to the living area and the inner courtyard, where I spent many hours playing games with my little brother, Arnold, and my cousins, Magda and Zulik. Magda was two years older than I was, and Zulik was three years younger. The youngest of us all was my brother Arnold, who was five years younger than me. Despite his tender age, he insisted on joining us. His rollicking laugh accompanied the many hours we spent together, usually on the weekends.

My brother Arnold, age 3

Grandpa and Grandma's grocery store was in the front of the house. They sold general merchandise and were open during the day. The store entrance was from the street, and on my way home I would often stop there. Our residence compound was expansive and illustrated my family's financial solidity.

At that time, there were few residential apartment buildings in town. Upper floors were constructed only in buildings with various government offices or for houses of the very rich. Several wealthy Jewish families built two-story 'palaces' in the city center. Our residential building, like most of the houses in the area, was one-story, and a few single steps led from the entrance to the residential complex, which was divided into several spacious apartments.

My grandparents allotted the space and my parents built our residential compound. My childhood home included a very large room, divided into two sleeping areas - one for my parents and one shared by Arnold and me. There was a spacious kitchen in the center of the house.

The heart of Jewish home life of that time was in the kitchen, which had a seating area and a large dining table. There were usually no special 'living rooms' in the houses and all family gatherings, both small and large, were held in the dining area. That is the reason the kitchens in the houses were especially large. There was also a practical reason for this. The cooking stoves made it the most warm and pleasant place in the house during the cold winter months. Our house also had small, coal-fired heaters, as well as larger ceramic stoves, over which the adults leaned to keep warm.

Refrigerators were not yet in use when I was a child. People produced their own dairy products at home, or had them delivered to the house by milkmen. I remember a time when my parents kept a cow in a small barn at the edge of the yard that they milked for home consumption. Later on, they would buy dairy products from the milkman, who made his way between houses in the town.

Like many women in those days, my mother stayed at home and did not go to work. I remember running home at the end of the school day and from the far end of the street sniffing the aroma of freshly baked bread my mother had made. There were bakeries in town, but in most cases, we baked our own bread.

In those days, most houses in the city did not have running water. Behind the building was a well, and we filled buckets with water that came out of the nearby spring. There were also no indoor toilets. They were in a separate outhouse in the yard.

We had a house cleaner who was like one of the family. Her name was Maria, or Aunt Marie (Mari-neni). She was a 35-year-old non-Jewish woman who lived in the city and helped mother with household chores. Laundry, for example, was complicated, with no running water. On laundry day, Maria would come and fill water from the well in a special wooden container designed for this purpose, and it was kept in the storehouse. It was like a huge tub and inside of it it was customary to put a cleaning powder that had been previously heated from the ashes of the stove. After cooking, a kind of bleach formed from the ashes and the clothes were scrubbed and washed several times. In the summer, laundry day was held in the yard, and in the winter, everything was done inside in the kitchen, next to the wood-burning fireplace.

Maria also came every Saturday to perform activities forbidden for Jews on the Sabbath. Every week, early in the morning, Maria would come and turn on the stove to heat the stew my mother had made ahead of time. The smell of broth would spread throughout the house and whet our appetites.

Thanks to Maria, we were able to have heat on Saturday morning. The heating stoves were lit every day, but we turned them off at bedtime to prevent a fire. During the night, the rooms were kept warm from the heat of the stoves even after they had been turned off. On Saturday, we were prohibited by the Sabbath from lighting the stoves. Maria was our 'Shabbos goy' and would come in Saturday morning to relight the fire and add wood every few hours to keep it burning. My parents left a pile of wood for this purpose on Fridays, to make sure the fire would heat the house all day Saturday.

The use of a 'Shabbos goy' was common in Berehovo, as almost all the Jewish families kept the Sabbath, and the houses needed heat and a fire to be lit every day during the winter.

As I said, our backyard was very spacious and more than 100 meters long. A shed for storing wood was next to the courtyard, where we kept wood we used to heat the house in the cold winters. We also had smaller storerooms, full of all good things, where we kept preserves during the summer, including canned vegetables, pickles and jams.

Further down the yard was a vegetable garden where we all worked, mostly on Sundays. Every year my family grew flowers in it, as well as onions, cucumbers, tomatoes, lettuce, cabbage, radishes, beets and more. When a season ended, we would hire a gentile to turn the soil over and prepare it for the next season. We all did the sowing and harvesting, together. I loved the joint work in the garden. These happy family memories are with me to this day.

As I mentioned, the garden was divided into several beds that included seasonal vegetables, which Mom cooked for us. Like all children, I loved my mom's food. I can picture our family: Grandfather at the big dinner table, Dad saying Kiddush, and the aroma of my mother's cooking delighting my senses. I remember the sauerkraut and another of my favorite dishes, a Hungarian cabbage dish of sweet and sour flavored peppers, which my mother would pickle and seal in a vacuum container.

On the street where we live in Ramat Gan there is a stall selling Hungarian food, including this dish.

Even today, at the age of 90, I cannot bring myself to eat it, though its taste has been with me for decades. Even the smell of this childhood favorite makes me tremble as I walk down the street.

In Berehove, there was one Hebrew kindergarten where I studied until the age of six.

My Hebrew kindergarten, before the war. I am second from the left in the front row.

Besides the formal education at kindergarten and in school, it was very important for the Jewish community of Berehove to educate the young children in the mitzvahs and to give them a close acquaintance with Jewish religion and customs. From age 5 in the afternoons most Jewish boys went from kindergarten to the 'heder,' which was next to our house, and studied Judaism until the evening hours. The teachers were rabbis and there were several 'hederim' in the city, divided according to age. The older children studied Gemara and Jewish history. We younger children studied various religious subjects.

When I graduated from kindergarten, my parents enrolled me in the regional Czech school, which was located in a spacious compound in a part of the courtyard of the city's great synagogue. I attended this school from age six to age 12.

The school was in the city center far from home, and every morning we walked for about twenty minutes to get there, in all kinds of weather. Although the city was flat and in our free time, we often rode our bicycles, we always walked to school. The lessons were conducted in the Czech language and, like most any child, I preferred the painting and art classes to the 'regular' subjects.

At school, they called me 'Ludwig,' my secular name. Every Jewish child has both a Hebrew and a secular name, which we use in school and in non-Jewish public life. During the day, I was Ludwig, at home and in the afternoon religious school - the heder- I was Moshe. When I arrived in Israel my Czech passport had Ludwig written in it and the Aliyah people who picked us up wrote that name. I kept it that way so that in my official papers, in addition to my Hebrew name Moshe, the name Ludwig appears, just as it had accompanied me in younger days.

At home they called me 'Moishi,' and this was my favorite.

In the Czechoslovakia of my childhood we had no sense of being a minority. I had Jewish friends and Christian friends with whom I really enjoyed playing soccer. During this period, Germany issued the Nuremberg Laws (1935) and the situation of German Jews began to change, as new decrees were imposed on them at once. Life for us at this point still ran smoothly and our daily routine went on uninterrupted.

Around the age of eight, I went to study at Rabbi Itzkovich's heder, which was designated for the older children. We were the youngest ones there.

We would arrive right after the end of the school day and I remember we young children had a hard time staying focused and studying every day for so many hours in a row. Sometimes, as it happens with children, we disrupted the lesson. Our heder teacher used a stick made of flexible bamboo to knock on his desk to silence us. The stick was also often used to hit unruly students on the buttocks. We were afraid of the rabbi but despite his authority and our fear of punishment, I remember many times that we came up with clever initiatives to evade the possibility of him punishing us. One time we brought garlic cloves to heder and when the rabbi wasn't looking, we smeared garlic on the stick. When the rabbi banged the desk, the stick fell apart and we all burst out laughing. The rabbi's interrogations didn't work; no one would confess. The fact that these were childish pranks did not ease the teacher's anger. He was furious with us and imposed collective punishment on the class.

Our economic situation continually improved.

Dad set up a small, homemade farm factory for goose products. There was a scarcity of oil and every home needed goose fat for cooking. The factory also made foie gras, which was considered a delicacy, and the goose legs were smoked in a special shed set up for this purpose. The oil extracted from the geese was both for personal use and for sale, and was stored in an outdoor shed in the winter. No refrigeration was required; it was cold enough outside.

The goose feathers were plucked and the first layer was sold to Gentiles. We kept the second layer, with the better quality feathers, and used it as filling for blankets. Down jackets were not common then, and our warm clothes were made of pure wool. In general, there were no clothing stores. Everything was tailor-made and custom-fit. The neighborhood tailor would come to our home for measurements, or invite us to his workshop. Each of us would receive festive suits that we wore on holidays and Saturdays. The tailor would also sew us outerwear according to our size.

My parents also made special delicacies from duck fat. I remember a dish I particularly liked. On cold winter evenings we used charcoal from the oven and roasted skewers with pieces of goose fat seasoned with paprika and spices and chunks of meat. We all sat around the oven, making a loaf of fresh bread and holding the delicious smelling skewers in our hands. We were happy.

Since it was a small, home factory, the work was done manually to ensure the quality of the products, even though we already had electricity and could have used machinery. Dad worked diligently and the business grew. My father felt that with proper management it would be possible to realize the business potential of the small home enterprise and make it more commercial and profitable. He thought about how he could turn his home business into a larger family business.

Dad's sister, Malka, also lived in our city. I called her Aunt Mali, and her everyday name was Marie. She was married to Ignaz Lazarowitz. As was customary in Jewish families, the Lazarowitz family lived with Ignaz's parents near the city center. They owned a great deal of land and were very well off.

By joint decision of my parents, uncle and aunt, Dad moved the activities of the home factory to the compound where Ignaz and Aunt Mali lived, which was much larger. The joint venture they set up was industrial size, and contained all the meat processing equipment. Moreover, they would now also be able to make other products that were difficult to produce in the small home factory.

The meat was kosher, under the supervision of the local rabbinate, and the new plant had electrical machinery so that production was more industrial and substantial, compared to the manual labor used until then. In addition, the factory was in a more central location in the city: close to the Great Synagogue and in an area bustling with commercial activity.

Once they merged the two branches, my father went to work in the new factory, which prospered.

Malka and Ignaz had four children: Moshe, Barry, Ilona and Magda. My cousin Moshe had completed his schooling and worked with my father in the factory. They both saw the potential of the home business.

The two families had an even warmer relationship than before, due to their working together.

In the course of time, my cousin Moshe would be the first family member I would see after my release from Buchenwald at the end of the war. However, at this point in the story, our meeting is still far off in the future...

The 1938 wedding of my cousin Yuli Lazerovitz.
My parents and grandparents are either side of the bride and groom. My parents are third and fourth from the left in the back row.

Other relatives who were very significant in my childhood years were my uncle and aunt Isidore and Rosie Kessler.

Isidore was my father's brother and they lived near us. Isidore and Rosie had three small children, and the two families had a warm and close relationship. Isidore worked in a meat processing plant in the city, and in addition, his family ran a clothing and textile shop on Berehove's main street, Andarshi. We called the shop 'The Corzo.'

My aunt Hani, who lived in our compound, worked in the shop with Rosie. The two women made embroidered products and sold them there. The store's central location on Andarshi Street, the city's main street, where there were many cafés, contributed to its success.

Although I was born in the city, from a young age I liked open spaces.

Close to our house was a large natural lawn, where they sometimes held horseracing and sports competitions. For us kids, it was a soccer game paradise, and we would play there many hours running around carefree. In the more out-of-the-way area of the field were gypsy camps.

We were all waiting for the moment when we would get bigger and be able to take part in the Zionist youth movements that operated in the city and go on the nature trips the movement organized. Starting in 1930, most of the Jewish youth in Berehove had joined the Zionist youth movements. At first, it was the Scouts, then Hashomer Kadima, Betar, Hapoel Mizrahi and Hashomer Hatzair. The members walked around the city in the afternoon in their uniforms, proud and happy. When I was about 10, one of my older cousins took us along and we joined an activity of the movement every

Friday. I loved participating in the activities. In our house, we took great pride and had a deep sense of belonging to the Zionist initiative. I especially remember the song "Hatikva" which echoed throughout the hall where the activities took place.

Unfortunately, by the time my friends and I reached the right age to join the movement, life had changed completely.

Another place I really enjoyed visiting as a child was our relatives' house in Ardo, a quiet suburb of Bergsas, which was more countryside in nature. My father's sister, Fanny, lived in Ardo with her husband, Zvi Marmelstein. They had four children older than me: Abraham, Moshe, Rachel and Margit. Mom and her sister Hani often went to see Fanny, and took Magda, Zulik, Arnold and me with them.

They had a pub in the yard, and the family made a living from it. In the backyard was a kind of bowling alley on the grass, where we used to play with the neighbors' children.

When I was a boy, winter was our favorite season. We waited impatiently for the first snowstorm, which coated the city in white. Every year the sight of the first snowfall excited us as if it were the first time we had seen it. Everything was pure white and when we wore our warm clothes; the cold did not bother us at all.

The city streets were covered in ice and we all ran around, sliding in our shoes. Some of the streets were unpaved and in winter, they became a real paradise. On the colder weekends, we would go to lakes in the area, which were completely frozen. We tied special skates over our shoes to skate on the ice. These were among my most precious possessions on earth at that time. The straps wrapped around our regular shoes and tightened with a key.

Arnold at 4 ½ and me at 9 ½ years old, in our backyard.

Even inside the city there were frozen surfaces we skated on for hours. The river that cut through the city also froze over, and at a certain point we could skate on that too. The rolling laughter of children could be heard from a distance, and our parents had to muster up all their authority to get us to leave the white spaces around us and make us come home in time for dinner.

Years later, when the war ended and I was preparing to immigrate to Israel, I found on the farm where we lived in the Sudetenland a key for skates, like the one I used to have at home. A twinge of pain and longing gripped my heart. I took the key with me; it always reminded me of my happy childhood days, before the war…

Despite my great love for winter, like any child I looked forward to summer vacation. Our city was flat and our main means of transportation - children and adults alike - was on bicycles. My parents preferred to walk, but my friends and I enjoyed riding around on our bikes. During the summer and also on holidays it was easier to meet friends from school thanks our ability to pedal quickly to anywhere in the city.

Every summer I would spend a lot of my vacation with my grandparents and my mother's parents, grandma and grandpa Blubstein, who lived in Dobřenice. By train it was not very far, and my mother would go see her parents for about a week during the summer vacation every year. I would go with her and remain at my grandparents' house in the village for a few more weeks.

Grandpa and Grandma Blubstein lived on a small farm near the village train station and I loved staying with them. Animals roamed freely in the farmyard, especially chickens and cows, and the quiet village life fascinated me as a child. Arnold was still too young to be away from home, and I got all the attention from my grandparents and enjoyed the treats they showered on me. I especially liked the big fresh loaves of bread, which were typical among families in the villages. The bread had a sour taste, similar to the sourdough bread we have today.

Mother's younger sister, Iren, lived in the village with her grandparents. Even though she was my aunt, she was only three or four years older than I was. Iren and I had the best time together, romping in the fields and running in the open area around the farm, the nearby springs and woods. We used to go for long walks in the woods, picking wild strawberries and raspberries and gorging ourselves on them until we got stomachaches.

A short walk away behind the train station was a mountainous pine forest. The path through it led to a high plateau with clear, cold springs of water. Every day, we would go to fetch water from the springs for the house.

Behind the house, there was a vegetable garden and further on, a beautiful blue stream from the Hong River. I loved swimming in the river with Iren on hot summer days. The water was freezing but very refreshing and we had the best time.

One of Grandpa and Grandma's neighbors, Mr. Jutkowicz, owned a butcher shop and his house had a large yard full of fruit trees. Jutkowicz spent most of his time in the shop and Iren and I loved to wander around the big yard, with his permission. I especially liked the apple-picking season when the trees were heavy with fruit. We would bang a nail into the end of a long stick and get the juicy fruit off the tree branches. I still remember the wonderful taste of those apples even now.

In all the houses near my grandparents' house lived Jewish neighbors who engaged in the food business and grew fruits and vegetables in the yards of their homes. Nearby was a spacious field where the neighbors prepared dried grass for the winter to feed the animals. The hay had a very special smell, which stayed with me long after the last time I visited my grandparents.

Years later, when I was already an adult, I would stop during one trip or another in Europe near the vast fields in Austria or Switzerland to smell the dried hay and conjure up in my imagination the happy childhood days in Dobřenice.

When I was six or seven, my grandmother passed away. Despite my young age, I remember my mother's trip to the village to sit Shiva for her mother. Mom invited my grand-father to stay with us but he preferred to stay in the village with his youngest daughter, my aunt Iren, because there were animals on the farm that needed to be taken care of. Iren, who was only a few years older than me, helped keep house after my grandmother died. Sometime later, Grandpa remarried.

Many of the things I experienced then as a young child, both in my city and in the village, are still engraved in my memory today.

Unfortunately, I have very few pictures of my parents' house and from my childhood. In those days, family photog-raphy was not a matter of routine, and involved considerable financial outlay. Most families could not afford to be photo-graphed professionally. The landscape and the expressions on the faces of my family are forever etched in my mind.

Ever since I made Aliyah to Israel, I have never once had the desire to return to Berehove to walk the streets of my childhood and see my parents' home. The reason is the bitter and painful memories of when I returned from the camps and realized that the town I knew as a child had disappeared and would never be as it was, ever again.

Many of the people I knew as a child and many members of my family did not survive the inferno. Almost none of the Jewish-owned stores reopened when the war was over. The synagogues had been abandoned or ruined, and the vibrant city I had known was buried in the ruins of the war.

The only place from my childhood to which I would be happy to return is Dobřenice, the village where I spent so many happy days, and which has no painful memories for me.

When my thoughts wander to my early childhood – I regret that we did not know then to treasure every moment together – I breathe in the smells, concentrate on the sights, and the tastes that will never come back. If only we had heeded the few voices that tried to make us see the impending danger and warned us, crying out to us to flee...

A few years before the war, my grandpa Kessler fell ill. In those days, there were no antibiotics and complications of diseases such as pneumonia often led to death. Grandpa Kessler passed away at home, and I remember they took Arnold and me to Aunt Malka Lazarowitz's house when the funeral was held. We were there with the rest of children in the family and I was very sad. From the day I was born, my grandparents had been present in my life; in fact we all shared a common residence complex.

In retrospect, it is clear to me that Grandfather Kessler was spared enormous suffering and certain destruction by dying when he did.

My grandfather Zev Blauvstein before the war.

Berehove becomes Bergsas

Jewish life under Hungarian occupation

During 1939, when I was eight years old, the winds began swirling around us…

Hitler had already established his rule in Germany and began eyeing neighboring countries.

In March 1938, Germany annexed Austria. Hitler's next step was a demand for a return of the Sudetenland in Czechoslovakia to German sovereignty. He made Western countries believe that he had no ambitions for a wide-ranging war, but only wanted to annex the territories Germany lost in the World War that included populations of ethnic Germans.

Hitler's real intentions were not yet obvious, but it was already clear that he was a powerful and dominant ruler. It is important to understand that the countries of Europe were still suffering the trauma of the terrible First World War, and were determined to do all they could to prevent their countries from paying the horrific price of war again. The Prime Minister of Great Britain, Neville Chamberlain, feared that if Germany did not receive sovereignty over the Sudetenland, it would declare war on Czechoslovakia and the whole of Europe would be drawn into bloody battles against its will. Chamberlain knew that his nation expected him to prevent any possibility of Britain finding itself at war again.

The Prime Minister of France, Édouard Daladier, also believed that a policy of restraint and acceptance would appease Hitler, put his mind at ease, and provide the most appropriate response to the aggressiveness of the new German government. The prime ministers of Britain and France were determined to do whatever it took to prevent another outbreak of war, and Hitler took full advantage of that fact.

Hitler's real goals were not revealed at that time. His statements about his desire for peace were only a temporary cover-up, to disguise his plans for a full-scale war to institute the Third Reich in all of Europe.

The opening shot of World War II was actually fired by a diplomatic 'weapon' - the Munich Agreement signed in September 1938 between Hitler and the leaders of Britain, France and Italy. This agreement allowed Germany to annex without any objection the Czech Sudetenland, where many ethnic Germans lived.

It is important to note that Czechoslovakia was an independent state with military capabilities, a well-fortified border, and weapon factories that would help defend it against the German army. In addition, as part of the alliance signed by the various European countries, it was promised French and Soviet support in case of attack. Various studies show that at *this stage, the German army was not yet prepared enough to win the war, and it is possible that if Czechoslovakia had been given the opportunity to defend itself in the face of German aggression the future would have been different.*

However, historical events went another way, and Czechoslovakia's capabilities to defend itself against Hitler's territorial aspirations never materialized. Britain, led by Neville Chamberlain, pressured its allies to sign an agreement with Hitler that supported the German annexation. The sacrifice of the Czech state for the sake of a longed-for continuous peace was in retrospect a deadly mistake. It eliminated any possibility of saving Czechoslovakia and perhaps even the whole of Europe from the takeover by Nazi Germany.

So it was that the first step on the path to the most terrible war in human history was taken, ironically, in the name of peace.

All this had not yet affected us; it was like far-off news, but not for long.

The following occurrences had an almost immediate impact on our daily lives.

As I have already mentioned, Hungary had never come to terms with the loss of vast and fertile areas of Carpatho-Russia, and its overriding goal was to return this territory to the Hungarian state. Hitler promised Hungary as early as 1937 that it would regain the territories it lost in the Great War, later known as the First World War.

The annexation of the Sudetenland by Germany in 1938 prompted Hungary to take action and it demanded to take back sovereignty over the territories taken from it in World War I. In the arbitration agreement that took place in Vienna, they made a decision to return Carpatho Russia and other territories to Hungary.

Most of the inhabitants of the region were indifferent. Some even welcomed Hungarian annexation and easily bid farewell to their years of residence under the Czechoslovak flag in favor of "Great Hungary" as it was now called.

There were some Jews who at this point decided to flee and immigrate to Eretz Israel. Among them was Haim Blubstein, my mother's brother, and his girlfriend. The young couple became engaged and left Hungary by way of a circuitous, treacherous, and uncertain path. In 1938, the two managed to arrive in Eretz Israel illegally and escaped the cruel fate of the Jews of the area.

I will meet Haim and his wife again when I immigrate to Israel, in 1949.

In early 1939, unimpeded, Hungary annexed one-third of the area of Czechoslovakia, including Carpathian Russia - our area - and regained all the territories it had lost in World War I.

Without a single bullet fired, the Czechoslovakian country in which I was born disintegrated and virtually ceased to exist.

Our town's name changed back to Bergsas and we were now part of "Greater Hungary." I remember the teachers at school composing a sentence in Hungarian: "Greater Hungary is like paradise and Little Hungary is not a country."

In March 1939, the Hungarian army entered Berehove which, as mentioned, had reverted to its Hungarian name, Bergsas.

I was a young child and did not yet understand how significant this change would be in our lives.

The Hungarian government required all Bergsas children who had attended Czech schools to learn Hungarian from now on. I was now given a Hungarian name at school: Leyush. After the war, I took this name off all my documentation and made no further use of it. I tried to erase with it everything that had happened to us.

Over the years friendships flourished between Jews and Gentiles. The children and young people enjoyed going around the city without separation between the Jews and their neighbors.

After the Hungarian takeover, that began to change.

The economic opportunities created by Czechoslovakia were available to the general population, but were not taken advantage of in the same way. While most Gentiles regularly visited the taverns after a working day, wasting money, the Jews worked hard and took every opportunity to acquire an education and a profession that could improve their future lives. As a result, an economic gap grew between Jews and Christians, which led to hostility accumulating beneath the surface. It is important to note that many young Jews made a meager living and toiled, just like their neighbors. But the spotlight was on those who had amassed economic assets, gotten an education, and gained in status.

Feelings of hostility and jealousy in light of the economic success of some of the city's Jews started coming out during the Hungarian rule, which completely legitimized these feelings.

The Hungarian authorities were known to be anti-Semitic and there began more and more harassment of Jews in the areas where they lived. This harassment became more and more overt and institutionalized. That was a major change for us, as the Czech government and the Czech people were free of prejudice and there was no anti-Semitism during my childhood in Czechoslovakia. Moreover, the Czech people continued helping Jews as much as they could throughout the war years. This is in contrast to the Hungarians. Only a very few chose to help Jews and were awarded the title of Righteous Among the Nations.

Back to the new reality of our lives...

Hungarian Prime Minister Miklos Horthy was openly anti-Semitic and encouraged discriminatory decrees against the Jews. The atmosphere changed not only in the upper echelons of the state administration, but also on the street. Our Christian neighbors began to hurl insults and curses at us.

Gradually, our daily reality underwent a change.

The Hungarian authorities began to issue laws that restricted Jewish entry into public institutions and spaces. In addition, various guidelines narrowed our possibilities and prevented us from enjoying equal rights and opportunities.

At first, these restrictions came slowly, in order to obscure what was happening, but over time the new attitude towards the Jews became obvious and apparent. We were not allowed to practice the liberal professions, the gates of the universities closed to Jewish youth, and the oppression became more varied. In the months following the fall of the Czechoslovak Republic, the Hungarians gradually expelled Jews from all governmental and local offices, as well as from schools and hospitals.

By 1940, there was not a single Jewish teacher in the city. Occupational disadvantages and discrimination reached into many other areas of life: Jewish judges lost their positions, and the number of Jewish lawyers able to continue practicing the profession steadily decreased. Doctors and pharmacists mostly worked privately and discreetly.

The hostility of the Hungarian regime began to show itself in all spheres of life. The vibrant youth movements operating in the town were forced to continue their activities underground, as the Hungarians disapproved of the organization of young Jews. The familiar and safe streets of my childhood town became threatening, as overt and legitimatized anti-Semitism began to spread like wildfire.

There was an agreement between the city's Jews and the local education system that Jewish children would come to school on Shabbat but would be exempt from writing, so as not to disobey religious laws. I remember one Hungarian teacher who tried to insist that we Jewish children write on Shabbat and he became furious when we wouldn't. One day, this teacher took all the schoolbags of the Jewish children in the classroom, mine among them, and threw them out the window, saying we should all be sent to be cannon fodder for Hitler. It was a terrible insult.

We still did not understand where all this would lead...

Our non-Jewish neighbors and friends began showing us hostility as well: the local Christian population had begun to express reservations about any close contact with us. At first, these were one-to-one manifestations of distance and resentment, but gradually the separation became overt and total, characterized mainly by the gradual indifference of the local residents to their Jewish neighbors and friends. As the months went on we had to face with grief and pain the loss of long-standing friendships that disappeared without any prior warning or reason that we could fathom. For years, we had walked together to school, spent vacation time to-gether, danced at the same parties, and belonged to the same sports clubs... After decades, and perhaps even centuries of warm and pleasant cooperation and neighborly relations, we had become an undesirable minority among the general population.

Time passed and our condition worsened.

In 1941, the authorities conducted a census. In 1942, based on the census data, the Hungarian authorities required the

Jews of the area to show documented proof that their fore-bears had been residents of Hungary in 1855. Those who did not possess such proof were subject to deportation to the east - to Poland.

My mother's two older sisters, Miriam and Sarna, were married and their husbands' families and did not have the necessary documents to prove their "Hungarianness." They were deported to Kaminski Podolsk in Poland and at first, we had occasional letters from them. In 1942, executions by firing squads began in the area where they were living. After the war, we learned that Mother's sisters, along with their families had to dig trenches, were then shot, and fell into them.

None of them survived.

At the end of 1942, came a particularly harsh decree, which affected almost every Jewish home in the city.

The Hungarian government ordered all Jewish men aged 20-45 to enlist in the Hungarian army in Jewish forced labor battalions. Hungary was an ally of Germany in the war, and fought the Red Army, on its eastern border.

In the past, Jews would enlist with their Christian com-rades in the Czech army, but now only the Christians entered the regular Hungarian army. The government sent male Jews to 'special' labor battalions to aid the Hungarian army, some in Hungary and others in conquered lands. The objective was to control the territories taken from Russia with irrefutable strength and authority.

Most of the Jewish men were sent from Bergsas to the Ukraine to build fortifications and perform hard labor for the German army. They were under the direct supervision of Hungarian army soldiers, who treated them cruelly. Among other things, they sent Jewish battalions into minefields either by vehicle or on foot, to detonate the mines with their bodies. In the winter of 1942-1943, thousands of Jewish forced laborers froze to death, after marching approximately one thousand kilometers in the snow and freezing cold in a retreat from the front after a massive assault by the Red Army.

The Hungarian soldiers treated the Jewish forced laborers as slaves and behaved atrociously to them. Jewish conscripts knew that escape or defection meant that their families in Hungary would suffer, and they would also be putting the lives of their fellow conscripts at risk. As a result, the Jewish battalion members gritted their teeth and attempted to do the best they could in light of the grim reality.

Only a few hundreds of the conscripted Jews managed to survive the war.

Almost every family in the city had to send men and older boys to these battalions. It was a significant blow, but compared to the fate of the Jews of Poland at that time, our lives were still somewhat bearable. Some Jewish businesses in Bergsas even benefitted from an economic boom, and everyone hoped and tried to have faith that the war would soon be over, and that we had to hold on until the raging storm passed.

The Hungarian army took both single men and married men with children into the labor battalions.

My father was among them.

My father in the labor battalions of the Hungarian army

I was twelve years old when they drafted Dad. I do not remember much from the moment he was taken to the labor battalions. However, to this day, I can still feel the last hug he gave me before he left, and his request that Arnold and I try not to upset Mom and help her as much as we could. Yes, children in those days too could drive their parents crazy...

The day Dad left, I became the man of the house. I tried my best not to worry Mom and help her with whatever she needed. Initially, Dad came home on short, infrequent furloughs. I don't remember much about these visits, only the moments of parting.

My father's enlistment would have affected our family financially had it not been for my uncle Ignaz (Isaac), my father's partner. He was too old for the labor battalions, so the family enterprise continued to operate even without my father, and supported our family. Moshe, my cousin who worked in the business, was still home at the time. However, a year later, he was also taken into the labor battalions, and the factory closed.

Gradually, they prohibited all Jewish business activity.

Every summer until 1942, I went with my mother to visit Grandfather in Dobřenice. When my father went into the labor battalions, Mother had to stay home. My Aunt Rosie's parents lived in Kostrina, which was not far from Dobřenice. I would travel with my aunt by train and get off in Grandfather's village. He would meet me at the station, which was near his house, and I returned home the same way, accompanied by my aunt.

I continued going to the village for vacations even in the period when the earth was already trembling beneath us…

Those were moments of happiness in a world that was beginning to unravel.

My Parents

1943 saw even more significant anti-Jewish laws issued by the Hungarian government. These laws almost completely restricted our daily lives. The decree that affected me the most was their stopping us from going to school.

Another major restriction was a law issued by the Hungarian government that banned kosher slaughter. Virtually all of the city's Jews kept kosher, and they would not compromise on this fundamental issue.

When the supply of kosher meat ran out, the city's Jews had to find a way around the prohibition, at the risk of their lives.

A group of men led the animals to be slaughtered a few miles away to Ardo, a district away from the city center. There, away from all eyes, the kosher slaughter took place.

Ardo was a quiet, rural area where Dad's sister, Fanny Marmelstein, lived with her husband Herman and their children.

I visited there often with my mother and little brother as I mentioned before.

However, one day I went to Ardo to carry out a mission…

A large, special knife was required to perform the ritual slaughter. Hungarian army soldiers roved the roadways carrying out random searches. If they caught the butcher with the knife used for slaughter, they would arrest him immediately. I don't remember which of the adults came to me and asked for my help. He told me to wear long trousers and conceal the large butcher's knife. The grownups believed that the possibility of their searching a twelve-year-old boy was slight, whereas for an adult the chances were much greater.

I slid the large knife deep in my pants pocket and walked the few miles from the city to the slaughterhouse. I was taking a big risk, but I was not afraid. The community needed kosher food and I had to help. On our way back, we were indeed stopped by Hungarian police who asked for identification. After checking our papers, they let us go back to the city.

As you may recall, Dad's sister Mali's family, the Lazarowitz family, were partners in the factory until Moshe was taken into the Labor Battalions in 1943. The Lazarowitz children were older than we were, and my cousin Ilona, whom we called Ilo, was highly intelligent. She graduated from high school with top grades and moved to the big city of Munkács, where it was possible to go on to higher education. There, she studied to be a hospital nurse.

My cousin Ilona Lazarowitz

In 1943, when they issued the harsh regulations restricting daily life, Ilona realized that the situation in the area was dangerous, and it that would get even worse for the Jews. She decided that the best and safest place to spend the war was in Budapest. Despite her parents' objections against her leaving home alone at the age of nineteen in those uncertain days, she was determined. She wanted to leave Bergsas and work at the Jewish Hospital in Budapest. Ilona believed that the Jews in the city could more easily assimilate into the local population and not stand out, as they did in the smaller towns and villages.

Ilona also knew that there was a covert Zionist movement called the "pioneering underground" operating in Budapest, and that it had united several Zionist youth organizations in the face of the common threat to the Jews of Hungary. One of the members of the underground was David Gross (later David Gur), director of the Zionist Youth Association, who worked vigorously in the workshop set up by the underground to forge documents and smuggle young people into Romania.

This was how the lives of many young men and women were saved. The underground actively opposed the collaboration of the Hungarian authorities with the Nazi regime, and helped many of the city's Jews to escape while it was still possible, even after Budapest was occupied by the German army.

As I stated, Ilona's parents did not understand her decision. Budapest was far away and they preferred that the family stay together. As part of the general uncertainty, my uncle and aunt feared for their daughter's fate if she went alone to the big city. They tried to dissuade the 19-year-old Ilona, but she stood firm in her decision. My cousin Ilo was the only one in the family who was educated, and had the keen sense to see what was coming and take action.

She was right. Although Budapest was under German occupation from 1944 and on, there were many places to hide and the underground saved many Jews in the city with forged documents by finding them hiding places and distributing food stamps to them. Ilona managed to avoid the atrocities that were our fate after the Germans entered Bergsas...

In September 1943, shortly after Ilona left, I celebrated my 13th birthday.

I had reached the age of observance of the Jewish tradition.

A photograph of me at 13, dressed in my school uniform.

I went up on the pulpit to read my Torah portion in the synagogue near our home, two days before Rosh Hashanah.

In the past, our community held large, joyous bar mitzvah celebrations, but when I went up to the pulpit that day, there was no festivity or party.

This significant moment, which marked my entry into adult life, was devoid of joy.

Symbolically, this day reflected the sadness that would accompany me all throughout my teenage years.

The German army enters Hungary

March 1944

Shortly after my bar mitzvah, things got worse.

István Horthy, the Hungarian prime minister, was anti-Semitic and encouraged restrictions and decrees, but he refused to lend a hand to mass extermination on the basis of race despite pressure from Nazi Germany. In early 1944, as the Red Army advanced westward and it was clear that Germany was about to lose the war, Horthy signaled to Western nations that Hungary was interested in moving over to their side and stopping the alliance with Germany.

The Germans saw what was happening and feared that Horthy would join forces with the Red Army, which was advancing towards the Carpathian Mountains. The Germans knew there was a large concentration of Jews in Hungary and they wanted to send them to Auschwitz, where the industrial death machine was at its peak. The Nazi leadership in Berlin realized that it could not trust Horthy to cooperate and on March 19, 1944, German armies invaded Hungary.

The war was going to end soon and the Germans did not want to give up the opportunity to annihilate the Hungarian Jews. A Nazi puppet government was set up in occupied Hungary. Horthy was still formally responsible for running the country, but they circumvented his powers and carried out the operation to exterminate the Jews of Hungary without his cooperation.

The Germans acted quickly and the story of the extermination of more than 500,000 Hungarian Jews towards the end of the war is one of the tragic events of the Holocaust.

The method that had worked throughout Europe - the identification and registration of the Jews, isolating them from the general population, crowding them into ghettos and deporting them to the extermination camps - began to be applied to us as well. Unlike other places in Europe where news had been circulating and at this point there was a deeper understanding of what was happening, we knew nothing. Hungary was cut off, and up to then there had been no mass deportations to Poland, so there was also no one to come back and tell us what was going on.

The Germans occupied Budapest and demolished the Jewish hospital building where my cousin, Ilona, worked after she fled from Bergsas a year earlier. The hospital staff moved with medical equipment to a nearby Jewish school, and continued treating patients. My cousin was part of this team.

Meanwhile, in Bergsas, some sort of routine continued for us...

Even after my schooling stopped, I continued to go to a heder that gave us children some kind of educational setting. The last heder I was in was at Rabbi Greenwald's house where studies continued almost until the evacuation to the ghetto. We were already older and the studies were an on advanced level, a kind of a small Yeshiva.

The heder was next door to my uncle's house - the Lazarowitz family. I would visit them often after heder. They lived in a large and impressive compound, and were without doubt the richest and most established among our family members. After Ilona left for Budapest and Moshe was drafted into the labor battalions, my uncle Ignaz and my aunt Malka, along with my cousins Magda and Barry, remained at home. Barry was a student in Munkács and returned home after we were banned from school. My aunt ran the store on the street at the top of the city almost until it was time for our evacuation to the ghetto.

On March 31, the Gestapo entered Bergsas. We were doomed.

Without our realizing it, the chokehold had slowly tightened around our necks.

Immediately after the German occupation, we received new instructions that required us to walk around with a yellow Star of David sewn on our clothes. Rumors soon started that they were gathering the Jews in our area into ghettos to concentrate them and send them in an orderly manner to work. It is important to remember that at this stage only the elderly, women, and children remained in our community. There were no young people to actively oppose what was happening, and even if they there were - the feeling was that complying with the guidelines would allow us to survive until the end of the war. The most correct response then, we felt, was to bow your head and wait until the storm passed. We knew that by this time, the German army was retreating on all fronts, and the hope of a complete and imminent defeat of Nazi Germany was alive in our hearts.

But soon, harsh reality hit us in the face.

The new decrees included a total prohibition on entering cafés, traveling by train, attending synagogue and going out in the streets after 6pm. The regulations were strictly enforced and required total obedience.

And sadly, the Germans had a lot of help in enforcing their rules.

Many believe that the Holocaust of the Jews of Hungary was actually the fault of the Hungarian regime, which was quick to cooperate with Germany and hand over the Jews without any hesitation. The Hungarian census from 1941, which the Hungarian government willingly provided to the Germans, gave them the information needed to locate and identify the Jewish families quickly and efficiently. If there had been any delay in submitting data or refusal to cooperate, it would have made it harder for the Germans to carry out their plans.

Our Hungarian neighbors were full of a deep hatred towards us that had grown over the years without us being aware of it. After the German occupation, this hatred was felt full force. Among the Hungarian people, only a few agreed to conceal Jews and help them in their time of great suffering. Most Hungarians actively cooperated with the Germans.

Imagine the feeling...

We had lived side by side for decades. During World War I, Jewish soldiers fought together with their Christian friends and neighbors. Some fell defending the Hungarian homeland and hundreds of Jews received medals for their bravery in battle.

Although we were Zionists, we did not want to go and live anywhere else. This was our country, whether the regime was Czech or Hungarian. This was the only home we had ever known: our homeland, which we were willing to defend with our lives and for which many of us had died in past wars.

Only twenty-five years after the many Jewish soldiers of the First World War hung up their uniforms, their homeland turned its back on them and erased from its memory and consciousness the Jews who had fought for it. At best, some Hungarians disregarded the fate of their Jewish neighbors and friends. In most cases, however, they were full partners in the process leading up to the extermination of the Jews of Hungary.

Life in the ghetto

April 1944-May 1944

In accordance with the German plan, they gathered Jews throughout Hungary into ghettos. There was a local branch of the Nazi Gestapo in Hungary, and its members were happy to carry out the Germans' instructions with perfection. One day, in early April, a few days before Pesach, we were ordered to assemble.

Each community knew exactly who was Jewish. They had lists and it was not difficult to gather us all together. Our clothes bore the yellow badge, which made it even easier to identify us.

Looking back, the question arises: why did we go along with it? Why didn't we rebel against the orders to leave our home? This is a complex question in retrospect, but the answer is simple if we examine it through the perspective of those days.

The German methods prevented insurrection or refusal very simply. The authorities took local Jewish leaders - community officials and rabbis - and held them hostage. They were placed under heavy guard and word spread throughout the city that if the Jews refused to evacuate their homes, the hostages - whom we all knew - would be killed immediately.

The threat worked. In one or two cases, they executed hostages in our area anytime there was a delay in carrying out the instructions. In that way, total obedience was extorted from the people of the city.

You must understand that our future in those days was completely uncertain, for better or worse.

Our daily routine had gradually changed in the past two years, with each new directive or restriction by the Hungarian regime. We may even have thought that this was just another period of temporary worsening of conditions, and we would soon return to our homes.

Information about what to expect next was concealed in a way that dispelled our suspicions. It is possible that if someone had hinted to the Jews of our city that we were being led to our deaths, many of us would have gone into hiding to try to save our lives. Also, most of the Jews obeyed the orders because no information about extermination camps had reached us at that point. It is important to understand that facts that seem clear after the Holocaust were seen as impossibilities at the time. We felt we were doing everything possible to stay alive until the imminent defeat of Germany.

Even today, with all the knowledge we have and the testimonies of the Holocaust survivors who scorched the souls of the Jewish nation, it is still hard to believe that such atrocities actually happened. At that time, the combination of deliberate concealment by the authorities and the human instinct to hope that the future would be better led to obeying the orders. Very few Jews chose to take a risk and hide with local Christian families and only a few locals agreed to help them, even though in a rural area like the one where we lived there were many options for hiding.

Most of us, however, preferred to stay together and believed that disobeying instructions might result in death, while following orders and moving to a labor camp would allow us to survive until the war was over. Systematic German trickery worked well in combination with threats, which prevented us from any thought of refusing to obey.

After the arrest of the community leaders, an order was issued: we were forbidden to leave our homes for three days. The authorities made it clear that anyone who violated the order would die.

In the next few days, the Hungarian police raided our houses. Under the new law, Jews were forbidden to keep gold, jewelry, and other valuables in the house. Mom and I hurried to dig holes in the lumberyard to bury our silver and other valuables, as well as our best bedding. I remember being very active in the excavation and concealment process. Mother sewed all the gold we had in our clothes. I remember actively helping Mom hide our possessions and quickly get ready to leave our home.

When the order came to evacuate our homes and assemble, the Germans made sure to reinforce the rumors that they were doing this so they could send us to factories that needed workers.

The instructions about the move to the ghetto were conveyed in the usual way throughout the city: messengers on bicycles rode from place to place, with drums and portable speakers. Others stood at the main intersections and passed on the message, demanding that we quickly arrange to evacuate our homes. In the city center they placed large, permanent loudspeakers that also repeated the orders. We were not to take anything with us except personal belongings, a knapsack with some clothes, and some provisions for the journey. It was clearly a worsening of conditions, but not something life-threatening. Still, the prevailing feeling was that something very bad was about to happen.

After they ordered us to evacuate our homes, police officers from the Hungarian Special Unit came to each Jewish home to round up the occupants. In my mind's eye I can still see them. They went from house to house in their uniforms, and wore high hats with a feather on their heads.

The Hungarian policemen escorted us to the trucks that took us to the far side of the city. We were all together: Grandma Clara, my aunt Hani with Magda and Zulik, Mom, Arnold, and me.

I looked back at our beautiful new house. I was sorry to leave, especially when we did not know where they were taking us. I remember the expressions on some of the neighbors' faces looking out the windows of their homes. No one looked really sorry. I believe that their real sorrow came much later, when they saw that some of us had managed to return...

The Bergsas ghetto was established on the site of the brick factory, which was on the outskirts of the city, not far from the train station. All the Jews of the city were concentrated under the long sheds of the factory buildings. The place was huge. I knew that many of my Jewish friends and extended family were with us there, but I didn't have a chance to see them. My family members who moved to the ghetto included my uncle and aunt - Ignaz, and Malka Lazarowitz - and my cousins Magda and Bari. Isidore, my father's brother, had been drafted, but his wife, Rosie, and their three young children were there in the ghetto.

There was also Shani Itzkowitz's family. Our parents were cousins and Shani was my age. His Hungarian name was Shandor but everyone called him Shani. They lived on Akrazia Street, not far from us. Shani went to the Hungarian school, so we did not see each other on a regular basis. In 1942, Shani's father was also drafted and he came to the ghetto with his mother and younger brother. We did not see each other at that time, but later our fates will be linked together.

We got off the trucks at the factory, and settled into the long open-sided sheds that were used to store bricks. This was our home for the several weeks. The factory was fenced off and police officers were stationed there to make sure no one left. Although we were occupied by Nazi Germany, there were no Germans around at all during this stage. The entire evacuation process, the guarding and shepherding, was efficiently carried out by the Hungarian police.

The conditions in this makeshift ghetto were totally unfit to hold thousands of people.

Each shed was about 15 meters long and, as I mentioned, they were open on the sides. It was April and it was still cold. I remember how freezing the nights were. We covered the sides of the sheds with blankets to try to protect us from the cold, but they only helped a little.

Each family was concentrated in one section of the ghetto. We were with Grandma, and the Leizinders - Hani, Shlomo, Magda and Zulik, who lived with us in the compound. The community began to get organized. They set up a central kitchen in the main shed, where they tried to provide fresh and cooked food as best they could. I volunteered to help in the kitchen and so I passed the time feeling like I was contributing.

There were no showers in the ghetto; we had to wash ourselves in cold water - not a pleasure in April - but we all hoped this was temporary and that we would soon move on to a better place.

When we had been in the ghetto for four weeks, we also celebrated Passover there. It was so different: away from home, without any matzah. We tried to preserve a holiday atmosphere in these poor conditions without much success...

One day in the middle of May, orders came to leave the ghetto and transfer to the train station. They told us that there were trains waiting for us to take us to labor camps. Today everything seems clear, and one might think we should have been aware of what was happening and that we were wrong to obey. But there had never been anything like the Holocaust, and even in their worst nightmares the Jews of my city could not have imagined the horror that awaited us.

Although by this time news spread across other countries in Europe, we were completely cut off. We knew nothing about the train activity and the transport of millions of Jews from different countries to the concentration and extermination camps. Media communications at that time were poor, the Hungarian occupation came late in the war, and the deportation of Hungarian Jews was swift and decisive. There were no survivors that had returned home and could tell us the truth.

There were ghettos in Poland for several years until they were demolished, but in Hungary they existed only a few weeks before we were evacuated. If the Hungarians hadn't helped them, it is doubtful that Germany would have succeeded at this stage of the war in carrying out its satanic plot to murder a community of hundreds of thousands of people within a few weeks. In Bergsas or in the whole region of the Carpathians there were no 'Righteous Among the Nations.' Only a very few Hungarians offered any help to Jews before they were imprisoned in the ghetto.

The almost total collaboration of the Hungarian people and its contribution to the fate of the Jews of Hungary is one of the ugliest stains on the human race in the history of World War II.

In mid-May, Hungarian gendarmes began evacuating the ghetto. They beat women, old men, and children with rifle butts and batons to urge them out faster. No one had any idea where we were going. The police kept saying that we were being transferred to our place of work. The secret was strictly guarded.

Train tracks passed near the factory, which had been used for bringing produce into the factory area during the days when it was active. The carriages were waiting for us there. Every few days soldiers of a special unit of the Hungarian police came and evacuated the sheds designated for that date.

It was our turn. Upon leaving the ghetto we were told to put all the valuables we had brought with us into a large bucket. The Hungarian soldiers collected all the gold and jewelry, including wedding rings. Like many of the women, Mom had sewed most of our gold into the lining of the coats we wore and in some of the clothes we took with us. These disappeared later on, along with our clothes.

We arrived at the train station with some food and water. We were greeted by freight cars, and were told to board.

I remember there was chaos: crowds of people, and loud noise. Armed guards pushed us to hurry up and get on the train. The carriages were crammed to the limits, not another pin could be inserted.

We heard the sound of them locking us inside the carriage.

Very little light penetrated into the car. Mom, Arnold and I clung to each other in the dark so as not to be separated. I think Grandma, Hani, Magda and Zulik got on with us. Many other relatives were put on the trains but in the confusion and the crowds of people around us, we did not see them. Each train had many cars and the evacuation to Auschwitz was carried out in several different transports, so we were split up. We also had no news of our family in Dobřenice. I later learned that in the rural areas too, the Jews were loaded onto similar trains and taken to the same accursed destination… About which we still knew nothing.

After what seemed like an eternity while we were crammed like sardines in the carriages, the train began to move.

It was impossible to sit down or stretch your limbs in the crowded car. We tried to make ourselves a place where we could manage the trip. I remember the unbearable heat inside the locked car and the terrible overcrowding. It was hard to breathe - very little air got in and it felt like we were suffocating. Everywhere people were trying to find some-where to lay their bodies.

A bucket was passed among us that we used for defeca-tion. After it was full, people poured out its contents through a high, narrow slot. The stench in the caravan was sickening as the hours passed. The trip took a long time. We could not really tell how long, but I estimate it was two or three days. The little bit of light that came in was through a small, high opening in one of the sides - ventilation intended for animals.

We had no idea where we were heading or when we would reach our destination.

On the first night of our trip, when it got dark outside, some of the younger men in the car thought about trying to break the window and jump off. Most of the others objected because they were afraid that an escape attempt would make things worse for us. In any case, the chances of surviving that high a fall from the window of a moving train were extremely small. By a majority vote the idea was rejected. We preferred to believe the rumor that better conditions awaited us and that they were not going to separate the families.

The trip was long with some stops on the way. We did not receive food or water and I got extremely hungry and thirsty. The trip in normal conditions would have taken less than a day, but it was a freight train designed for transporting cattle and it was very slow. Also, during this period, the Germans sent Jews from all over Hungary to Auschwitz. The tracks were overloaded with trains and we had to wait on sidings several times on the way.

The food we had taken with us for the road was not enough and the drinking water ran out at a certain point. We were hungry, thirsty, and thought that our situation would improve as soon as the train reached its destination and stopped.

How wrong we were...

The Hell Named Auschwitz

Before we go on - a few words about the accursed place we had come to.

The name "Auschwitz" actually stood for three large camps and about 50 smaller ones, subordinate to the main camps.

"Auschwitz 1" was the oldest of them all and was established in 1940. The camp contained the main headquarters of the SS and the barracks of the camp administration.

It was officially called "Auschwitz." It was here that the initial experiments were carried out to kill people with Zyklon B gas. Auschwitz was also the place where Dr. Yosef Mengele performed his medical experiments, in the infamous Block number 10.

In October 1941, Auschwitz 2 was established 3 kilometers away. It was called "Birkenau|."

In this camp, the Nazis built most of the mass extermination facilities, where approximately one million European Jews were murdered. Birkenau was the largest concentration camp in the Auschwitz complex. In 1944, more than 90,000 prisoners were housed in about 300 primitive wooden huts.

The third camp, Auschwitz 3, was built in October 1942 and was known as |"Buna-Monowitz." It was located in a nearby industrial area and used for forced labor under extremely harsh conditions. The camp included 45 sub-camps, which operated around it. Most of the prisoners worked in German factories.

At its largest, the Auschwitz camp empire included 45 camps covering 40 square kilometers. The Nazis made sure to isolate the camps from the outside world to avoid any contact or transfer of information, thus preventing escape options almost completely. Each camp was surrounded by high, electrified barbed wire fences, with high guard towers scattered along them. In addition, the Germans evacuated all the villagers from their homes within 40 kilometers, and created another security zone where SS soldiers patrolled with submachine guns.

And thus, far from any probing eye or local population, the Germans were able to carry out their appalling plan.

1,300,000 people were murdered in the Auschwitz camps - most of them Jews.

By the time our train rolled onto the tracks towards Poland, the death machinery at Birkenau was going full blast. The Nazis were well prepared for the arrival of Hungarian Jewry and the task that lay before them: the rapid extermination of about half a million Jews before the arrival of the Red Army, which was advancing rapidly towards the west. Some of the preparations for our arrival also included faster and more efficient 'reception' conditions.

Until the evacuation of the ghettos in Hungary in May 1944, the trains arriving at Auschwitz unloaded their human cargo on the 'Juden Rampa', which was located between Auschwitz 1 and Birkenau. The ramp was about a kilometer and a half from the last stop in the lives of most of the passengers - the crematorium. The first 'selection' was held there briefly after descending the trains, and the Jews' fate was decided with a wave of a hand: who will stay alive (for now), and who will end his life in a few hours. Most Jews were sent for extermination right away and in order to save unnecessary paperwork were not even registered. Immediately after being considered 'unentitled' to live, they made their final journey in this life to the Birkenau Crematorium…on foot.

Those who had difficulty walking were transported in vehicles camouflaged as ambulances.

In order to be more efficient, Hungarian Jewry got special treatment. Before the first trains arrived on May 16, 1944, the Nazis had done intensive work on the tracks that made it possible for the loaded trains to enter Birkenau directly. In this way, the Nazis saved valuable time and could exterminate us faster.

Hence, when our train reached its destination we were already inside the walls of Birkenau, a short walking distance from the four crematoriums that operated in the death camp 24 hours a day, 7 days a week.

Let me pause for a moment...These memories are very difficult for me...

Auschwitz 2

Birkenau

The train stopped

We had no idea where we were.

Then the doors opened.

The carriages were much higher than the platform, and we had to jump. The older adults and young children needed help, and out of nowhere, strange-looking men appeared with shaved heads, dressed in striped garments that looked like pajamas. These men assisted those who had difficulty getting down from the car. They used clubs to push us and make us hurry. After a few days in the grim, stuffy carriage, I was glad to get out.

Outside it was a relatively cool and bright day.

I looked around, squinting from the sudden brightness of daylight. I saw an open expanse in front of me, and I could see buildings in the distance.

There were barbed wire fences and tall guard towers throughout the area.

The first thing I noticed was that there were no plants, no trees, no shrubs, or flowers.

It was the middle of May and Spring was in full bloom. But here everything was gray.

On the left, I saw the entrance gate to Birkenau where our train had entered. It would always symbolize the camp for me in the future: the entrance to a manmade hell.

Armed soldiers surrounded the train.

This was my first encounter with the SS. They stood on the platform armed with submachine guns and rushed everyone with shouts to hurry and get off the train. Some of the soldiers had large, ferocious dogs on leashes, which were barking incessantly.

Veteran prisoners ordered us to form two columns: men to the right, women and children to the left.

I stood on the platform with Mom and Arnold. Mom held on tight to both of our hands. There was no time to think, to absorb what was happening in the commotion and turmoil of thousands of exhausted people, terrified from what awaited them. I think Grandma, Aunt Hani, Magda and Zulik also stood in line with us on the platform, but I am not sure. It all happened so fast and the chaos, the confusion, the noise all around...

They told us to hurry and carry nothing with us. The small bundles we had brought remained scattered on the platform.

Arnold and I stood in the column of women and children, clinging to Mom.

Suddenly one of the strange looking bald men scurrying around the platform trying to get us quickly into two columns came up to me and whispered in Yiddish:

"Tell them you are sixteen and go to the right. Get away from your mom right away."

I stared blankly at him.

"Go, fast!" He said, looking around to make sure no one heard him.

"You have to say goodbye to them, now. Fast! Before you reach the head of the line." He added: "Trust me!"

Thoughts raced through my mind...

"No I don't want that...I am not leaving Mom."

I was only thirteen and a half, where would I go without her?

"How will she be able to take care of Arnold in this place without my help? And what is here, anyway?"

I looked at Mom. I waited to hear what she would say.

Happily, Mom did not want us to split up either. She tightened her grip on my palm.

The line kept moving forward.

The dogs around us barked viciously, straining to break free. They foamed at the mouth, continuing to snarl hungrily at the long line of people getting off the train.

After a few minutes, as the line moved slowly, the bald stranger came back, this time even more determined.

"Listen to me good! Quickly! You must not stay with your mother."

"You can help her a lot more if you go right into the men's column and say you are sixteen. Believe me. It is very important! You have to do it!"

Mom looked at me, with a hesitant look. Something about the assertive tone of this man, who was a stranger to us but telling us repeatedly with determination convinced her that it might be best to listen to him.

"If he is so sure, then go." she said.

I was still uncertain. The man did not explain himself and I hesitated.

The fact is that I was afraid to say goodbye to my mother.

The man repeated his words. Mom signaled for me to move to the right column.

When no one noticed, I hurried to the other line. My legs buckled beneath me and failed after the long journey in the difficult conditions on the train. My stomach growled with hunger; I hadn't eaten anything for two days.

As soon as I moved over to the men's column, I no longer could see where Mother and Arnold had gone.

I was alone.

In all the commotion around me, I had no family or friends with me.

In normal times, I might have cried, but mostly I remember the uncertainty and confusion.

The veteran prisoners around us had not yet told us anything.

By 1944, almost everyone knew the truth about Birkenau and the veteran prisoners could not believe that we knew nothing of what was going on, at such a late stage of the war.

As the line moved on I saw a young man I knew from our city, Yossi Richter. The rest were strangers.

We advanced little by little.

I saw a table at the end of the column where several SS officers sat.

Above them stood a handsome German officer with a penetrating gaze. He was tall and very impressive, dressed in an ironed SS uniform with many decorations on it. His black boots shone and on his belt was a threatening pistol. He stared at us closely, one by one.

I reached the head of the column. His dark eyes surveyed me.

"How old are you?" He asked in German. "Wie alt bist du?"

At the Czech school, we had learned German, so I understood...

I straightened up, trying to look taller than my age.

"Sixteen," I replied.

He raised his hand and his thumb tilted to the right.

I was selected to live.

I walked in the direction he indicated. I did not know then that the stranger, who risked his life by approaching me, had saved my life for the first time. At this point, we still did not know anything about the place we had come to.

Only in retrospect did we realize that the strange process we went through when we arrived at the camp was in fact a selection for life or death. Cut off from my family, I stood there, a thirteen and half year old boy, alone and completely responsible for my fate.

We were ordered to go to the right, and walked to the absorption and classification area of the camp.

Long, low wooden sheds stretched before our eyes.

We could see chimneys churning up black smoke in the distance. This did not seem strange to us, as we thought we would be working in industrial factories. We did not yet know that in Birkenau there was but one industry - the industry of death.

We kept walking, arriving at a compound known as "Canada" so named by the prisoners because Canada represented a land of plenty and all the Jewish belongings left on the train platform were brought there in trucks.

We first began hearing stories at the sorting center about the crematorium and the diabolical deception the Germans used to achieve maximum cooperation from the prisoners until the moment it was too late to resist.

The veteran prisoners told us that the elderly, the children, and the sick were destined for immediate extermination as soon as they arrived in Birkenau. When the crowds arrived at the entrance to the crematorium area, an orchestra played. The Germans reassured everyone by telling them that they are going to take a shower after the long journey before reaching the camp compound where they would meet family members who had gone in the opposite direction.

This encouraging information helped ensure complete cooperation. The doomed women, elderly men, and children entered the hall. There they were given soap and sometimes a towel and told to undress. In the large room, there were signs on the walls emphasizing the importance of body cleanliness and a warning not to forget the towels and the hook number on which their clothes were hanging. The Germans thought of every detail that would contribute to the satanic deception and the mass murder that was easier to carry out.

They hung up their clothes and continued to the next hall. Scattered on the ceiling were fake showerheads, which made the space look like a huge shower room.

There was a valve in the ceiling, which opened only after the door hermetically locked and through which a chemical compound called Zyklon B was sprayed into the room. Zyklon B was a pesticide that was used to exterminate "all types of pests."

When all those in the room were dead, the Sonderkommando entered, Jewish men wearing special gas masks. They took the bodies to their final destination: the crematoria. The Nazis exploited the Jews even after their deaths: gold fillings were removed, hair was cut off, and the ashes of the dead were used as fertilizer for the camp vegetable gardens and the surrounding fields.

The outside world could not possibly grasp what was actually happening in Auschwitz.

Young people, who had been educated in the morals of enlightened Western culture, who had learned manners and civility were now murdering hundreds of thousands of people who could have been their own parents, grandparents, brothers, and sisters. These same people could have been - and until a few years ago perhaps even were - their friends from university or elementary school. They murdered innocent, naïve young boys and girls who could have been their own little children or younger siblings. Even the brainwashing that the Germans succumbed to, and the labeling of Jews as subhuman, cannot explain the capability of normal people to murder in cold blood without a shred of human compassion.

We looked up again at the smoke rising from the tall chimneys, not far off...And refused to believe it. The truth is there was no time to think or probe into the meaning of this information. Maybe it was better that way.

We quickly realized that although they had let us live, any weakness, illness, disobedience to orders, or even a momentary whim of an officer meant an immediate death sentence. We had to struggle every minute of every day to stay alive.

We awoke every morning not knowing if we would be alive at the end of the day.

I realized that to survive in Auschwitz I would have to keep a low profile and not stand out. It was the first instinctive behavior I developed there.

We tried to absorb only what was happening to us. We intuitively closed our minds to any other thoughts.

They put us in one of the barracks and veteran prisoners beat us with batons, urging us to undress quickly. They ordered us to throw our clothes, and socks and shoes on the floor in the middle of the hut. After we undressed, apathetic-looking inmates ran a rusty razor over our heads. It was very painful. These 'barbers' worked quickly and roughly, tearing hair right out of the skull. People around me began to lose their personal identity. Without hair and clothes, we all looked the same, and we became a collective mass of what had been distinct, individual human beings.

I don't know if it is even possible to imagine the situation we were in.

They kept us there naked for several hours. I was surrounded by a large group of strangers. At our age, we would usually be embarrassed to expose ourselves and would normally be seeking privacy. They denied us this right, along with so many others.

I do not remember feeling any emotion. I believe our senses were numb. The fact is, we did not even think about what had happened to our families. We were engrossed totally in trying to endure the new existence they had forced on us, completely cut off from everyone and everything we had known before. They had turned us into robots who follow instructions, devoid of human feeling and the motivation to do anything but obey.

After several hours, the guards herded us naked to another hut, where we were disinfected and sent to take a hurried shower.

It was freezing cold when we finished. We had no towels or clothes. The month of May in Poland is still very chilly, especially towards nightfall. We ran wet to yet another hut where they kept the clothing. In the middle were long tables with mountains of clothes piled on them. We passed along the tables as prisoners threw at each of us a pair of pants, a shirt, socks, a coat and a hat.

Naturally, the sizes were not right. They gave big-bodied people tight shirts and pants they could not even get into, while they threw the extra-large sizes at the older boys. We hurried to make changes among ourselves, and get ahold of clothes that fit our measurements as much as possible.

From the clothing warehouse, they led us to a large wooden barracks with a mud floor. There were two-tiered bunks inside. It was very packed, but I was glad to get to lie down and rest my sore limbs a bit after the cramped and crowded conditions on the train, where we had spent the past few days.

I fell asleep immediately.

Our first night in Birkenau...

Auschwitz 1

The next morning we marched the three kilometers that separate Birkenau from Auschwitz. When I say we 'marched,' try to picture vicious dogs barking at us threateningly, armed SS men screaming at us to go faster, and a profound and utter sense of fear.

When we arrived at the camp, they had us stand for a brief moment in front of the famous entrance gate. I tried to fathom the inscription above it – "Arbeit Macht Frei" - "Work Makes You Free," in German.

Compared to the wooden huts in Birkenau, the ones in Auschwitz seemed finer: neat rows of concrete buildings, and each sleeping hut had two-tiered bunks, so there were fewer people. There were even flowerbeds scattered here and there.

They took us to the showers. The Germans feared an outbreak of disease, so every time we went from camp to camp they sent us to shower and change clothing. After the shower, they ordered us into Block 16, where we would spend the next few days.

"Moishie!" I heard a voice call to me. I turned to see before me my friend and family member from Bergsas, Shandor (Shani) Itzkowitz. Shani and I were the same age, born two months apart. My mother was his father's cousin, and I sometimes saw him on family occasions. We did not go to the same school, but our families lived not far from each other and I knew him well. How happy I was to see him!

It turned out that he had been transported to Birkenau from the Bergsas ghetto shortly before me. The veteran prisoners had advised him to say he was 17, and to bid goodbye to his mother and younger brothers, just like I did. We decided that from that moment on, we would stay together and help each other survive, no matter what. We took the second tier on the bunks and filled each other in on all that had happened.

As we were chatting excitedly, they called all the prisoners in the block to come out. The guards took us to the administration area, and led us into a room where they recorded our personal details. A table stood in the middle of the room. Two men sat behind it, wearing prison uniforms, like ours. When it was our turn, they ordered us to extend our left arm. With special needles dipped in ink, they engraved a number into the flesh of our forearms.

This was our new name. The process, by which we lost our individual human identities, was complete. We were now a number...

The Germans did everything to demonstrate that they did not see Jews as part of the human race. This dehumanization process was consistent and always shocking. After being thrown into cattle trains, numbers were 'branded' on our skin, just as they branded cattle. This humiliation and degradation broke many of us, not only physically but also mentally.

We all looked the same. We lost every individual distinction: all with shaved heads, wearing bizarre, striped 'pajamas' that hung on our bodies in a ridiculous way, wearing identical caps and a blank expression in our eyes.

In Auschwitz, I was no more a 13 and a half-year old boy named Moshe Kessler.

I became A-4913.

Shani was right behind me in the line. He became A-4914.

Only a few months before we were two young friends with large loving families, friends, and plans for the future. We had a warm bed, and we never knew hunger.

From now on, we were two numbers. No identity, no sense of belonging, no family.

Lost and alone in the world, we had only each other.

We had no inkling of what had happened to our mothers and younger siblings, or where our fathers were. We knew that they are all most likely dead and tried not to think about it.

The past was gone as if it never happened. We knew instinctively not to yearn for the old days, or to think about them.

The future looked menacing with no hope in sight.

We went to sleep. It may sound odd and incomprehensible, but in the fight for survival and adaptation to the new and terrifying situation, it was impossible to think of others. Each of us was self-absorbed, dealing with the moment. We struggled only to survive and get through one day and then the next. We were in constant terror that we, too, were doomed to die.

In a sense, we had become animals in a human jungle, fighting for our lives with all our mental capacity - the only weapon we had left. My body was getting weaker and I knew I had to keep my spirits up and do everything I could to stay alive until the war was over and the nightmare would end.

The next day began our exposure to the daily routine at the camp.

The diet was miserable and we were hungry all the time. In the morning they gave us black coffee. Of course, this was not real coffee but a brown liquid that resembled it. At noon, a portion of thin soup without meat or potatoes, and in the evening sometimes only coffee and occasionally a thin slice of bread with some kind of spread on it.

Every morning and every evening we had to stand in queues for long hours, where they counted us again and again.

Auschwitz was not just a name of a place. It was a planet completely cut off from this world, with its own laws. We were haunted every day and every hour by knowing that at any second they could send us to the place from which no one returns.

After about a week at Auschwitz, they told us that we were leaving for a labor camp.

Relief washed over us at the news that we were about to get away from the tall chimneys with smoke spewing out of them day and night.

The Łagischa Labor Camp

We departed Auschwitz at the end of May.

They called out our names - or to be precise, our numbers. We were about a hundred men. They herded us into trucks and transported us to a small sub camp about a two-hour drive away. This was Lagischa.

Leaving Auschwitz 1 alive meant that for now the Nazis still saw us as useful to them. As long as you had value, your chances of survival were better. But even in the labor camps a death sentence still hung over our heads. The Germans held 'selections' arbitrarily, and those who were judged unfit for work were sent to the gas chambers at Birkenau.

The conditions in the labor camps had their daily effect. Many prisoners died of disease, starvation, the cold, and exhausting work under harsh conditions and in poor health. This was in addition to the sporadic individual and collective punishments they inflicted on us without warning or reason. By now I understood that our lives as Jews were as worthless as a garlic peel and that there was no certainty that this living nightmare would ever end.

The main and crucial advantage of the labor camp was that organized mass extermination was not actively carried out.

Łagischa was a sub camp of Auschwitz 3 (Monowitz-Buna) - Auschwitz main labor camp. It was a relatively small camp and most of the 700 inmates there were Jews from Poland, Yugoslavia and Hungary. A few were non-Jewish Poles and Soviet prisoners. In August 1944, a month before it was dismantled, there were about 700 prisoners in the camp, housed in four long barracks. Adjacent to these barracks was a medical clinic, and three additional huts served as warehouses. About thirty-five SS men guarded them day and night.

The Nazis had planned to set up an electric power station there for the German company EVO and worked the prisoners mercilessly to build it.

The prisoners carried out various physical tasks intended for the building of the power plant: the laying of railway tracks, digging ditches, and unloading machinery and building materials.

The trucks dropped us off at the entrance to the camp where we were met by the camp commander, Horst Czerwinski, a 22-year-old Pole who had enlisted in the SS. He was known to be a cruel and ruthless sadist. Czerwinski came to us after spending a period in the Birkenau extermination camp, and he made certain to make our lives miserable. Some prisoners were abused for no reason; others were murdered in cold blood.

They split us up into barracks like the ones in Auschwitz; concrete blocks with rows of two-story bunks inside. Each block had a "Blockmeister," a man in charge. Shani and I were placed in block number 3, and the person in charge of our block was a Pole with a slight limp named Yank Henig.

The camp was not crowded and relatively clean. As a result, we did not suffer from epidemics.

Compared to other camps, our conditions were relatively reasonable but the fact that the camp was run and controlled by a particularly cruel man and a cold-blooded murderer made us live every day in utter terror.

Czerwinski's looks were misleading. He was a tall, handsome man. Nothing in his face betrayed his monstrous personality. Evil is not always hinted at by external signs, and often the cruelest Nazi murderers were deceptive in their meticulous and ordinary appearance. If I had encountered them in any other situation I would most likely have been impressed by their character, without any idea that within them lurked a malicious devil.

The daily routine in Lagischa was identical to all the other labor camps in the Auschwitz complex:

The mornings started at about 4:30, while it was still completely dark outside. They shouted for us to report to roll call, which was held in a designated square – the Appellplatz. It was a nightmare for all of us inmates. We had to stand in straight and motionless rows twice a day: in the morning and immediately after returning from work. The roll call included counting and repeating exercise drills with our hats, for the amusement of the commanders.

The shortest time a roll call would take would be about an hour. In cases where the head count did not match or there were other reasons for delay, we sometimes stood there for four hours while individual columns of prisoners were harassed and abused by the camp commander and his officers. The fact that the camp was small was to our disadvantage, as the cruel camp commander was present at every roll call and involved in everything that was going on.

The roll calls took place in all weather conditions. Luckily, we arrived in Lagischa at the end of May, when the weather was relatively pleasant. Shani and I hoped that the end of the war was coming soon and that we would be spared the harsh winter.

I did not know it then, that it be would be ten more months until the day of my release.

We did our best to stay fit for work even on days when we had a hard time getting up on our feet. If you were sick at roll call it often meant an immediate death sentence from the camp commander.

Czerwinski always used to wear leather gloves. To this day I remember the gesture he made when he would look at us and play with the gloves. He liked to mistreat prisoners regularly and during the daily counts, he would look for anyone who did not seem fit for work. He asked that prisoners who did not feel well or had any complaint to approach him. We quickly learned not to fall into his trap.

When a sick prisoner approached, he was savagely beaten. In most cases the cruel game would begin with a fist waving in front of the prisoner's face. He would then send many of the sick prisoners to the shower area in the camp, and told them to wait there. When the parade ended, Czerwinski arrived at the showers and shot them all with his pistol. He then threw the bodies into the fire.

I think one of the hardest things about this period was knowing that regardless of our tenacity to survive until the war's end, our lives were in the hands of a cruel and bloodthirsty man, and we were subject to his mood any given moment.

After the roll call, they distributed breakfast - if you could call it that: a tiny, square bit of bread as dry as sawdust, with a small lump of margarine made from chemicals - nothing like the margarine I knew from home. At the end of this 'meal' we started the work day.

They split us up into groups and assigned everyone a work detail.

The satellite camps of Auschwitz 3, Lagischa among them, were scattered in areas where the Germans could build large industrial plants. Jewish forced laborers were the main workers at these plants at that time. Shani and I were assigned to a group of inmates working in a cement factory in the industrial area near the camp, to which we walked every morning.

The working day consisted of long hours during which we were forbidden to stand still. Anyone who stopped work for no reason was shot on the spot. There was no orderly break period and we did not receive any food the whole working day. From our meager 'breakfast' at dawn, we ate nothing until the evening.

We worked by unloading cement wagons near a Siemens factory. It was hard physical labor. Twelve hours a day every day, we hauled pipes and unloaded wagons full of heavy bags of cement. Our poor nutrition showed, and by this time I was a scrawny, hungry and weak boy. I was not yet fourteen and had to haul 50 kilo bags of cement most of the day. Thinking back, I don't know how I was able to carry such weight, especially in my fragile physical condition. We were so hungry that during the day, despite the risk, we tried to search in the bins of the industrial area, hoping to find scraps of food. We found nothing.

We returned to camp every evening. After the long hours of hard work, roll call awaited us and only when it was over did they give us any 'soup'. It was muddy water, food not even fit for cattle let alone for human consumption. Here and there, if you were lucky, bits of potato floated in the water. It was our only food. At an age when the body is growing and maturing, when the appetite becomes especially strong, hunger had its effect on our bodies, and we quickly became emaciated.

At the end of the evening meal we scurried to our huts. We collapsed there every night into a restless and dreamless sleep. Our heads were void of thoughts. Only primal instinct kept me alive in those days.

I had to survive, no matter what…

Thoughts were our enemies, as were feelings and longing. Dealing with the past was too hard, we lived the present. I was focused on trying to hold on to life, and not break down. Without being aware of it, I did everything to protect my young soul in the face of the terrible reality that threatened to crush it.

After a few weeks, one of the commanders took pity on us because we were still children, and assigned us an easier job.

Not far from the camp was a spacious vegetable garden and Shani and I were assigned our new job there. We had to tend the garden: to plant, pick the vegetables, and more. It was not particularly hard. Every morning we left the camp in threes, accompanied by SS soldiers with drawn weapons, and walked the few miles to the large garden we had to cultivate.

This became our daily routine for several months.

The Germans did everything to break any element of human individuality or uniqueness and made sure we remained a mass of nameless creatures. We looked the same, dressed the same, and were a row of numbers in a column. No one knew the others' names. At the line-ups and for everything else, they called us only by the numbers tattooed on our arms.

To maintain a uniform appearance we were required to report weekly to some inmates, who had old and unsharpened razors passed over our heads and shaved off the little bit of hair that was just beginning to grow. The process was dry, without water or shaving cream, and was excruciatingly painful. A prisoner without his hair shaven was severely punished. Luckily, as a young boy, I had no hair on my body, but for the adult prisoners the process hurt much more.

To keep order and spread fear as a deterrence, the Germans severely punished any violation of instructions. Despite this, some prisoners tried to think of ways to escape from the camp. I admit that I never thought of running away, perhaps because I did not see any possibility to succeed. We knew that any escape attempt would mean an immediate death sentence and we did our best to endure and try to survive.

Some prisoners tried to steal from the camp vegetable garden. We were so hungry all the time, so it was a great temptation. Some of us could not stand it, though it was clear that the person caught would be shot dead. The corpses of the 'criminals' who stole and paid for it with their lives were displayed at the entrance gate to the camp.

One day we heard that one of the prisoners who worked in the vegetable garden had stolen a potato. According to the strict rules, they executed any apprehended thief. When we returned from work, we found the perpetrator's body on a stretcher leaning against the camp gate. They hung a sign on it: "This is the fate for anyone who steals a potato." Even today, 76 years later, the grisly scene sticks in memory.

One morning an SS officer came and called out my number and the number of one of my friends, Naftali Greenberg. He ordered us to go with him, without any explanation.

My heart began to pound. Fear flooded my body. The unwritten rule in the camp said that as long you kept yourself unnoticed you were somewhat protected. We all knew that any call out of our number or absence from the workday was ominous, especially if an SS officer summoned us.

The officer who called me was a Hungarian, who had enlisted in the SS. We knew this because when they counted the prisoners, each officer did it in his mother tongue, and this one counted in Hungarian. He marched us quickly to the camp headquarters, a compound we were prohibited to enter, and ushered us into one of the offices.

On a table in the room were two bowls full of soup and next to them a piece of bread, for each of us. The Hungarian officer ordered us to sit down and eat, went out, and closed the door. Naftali and I stared at each other. We did not ask unnecessary questions; hunger overcame our fear and we quickly devoured the contents of the bowls and the bread. After some time, the officer returned and led us back to the barracks. Even today, I do not know why we were chosen. It may have been a completely random act.

I understood the significance of the event only many years later.

The camp commander realized that the war was winding down and decided to prepare a defense for himself for the day when it would be over. The Hungarian officer who called us for food had carried out the orders of Czerwinski, who believed that through this act he could claim to have taken good care of the prisoners and even saved the lives of two young Jewish boys. He thought this would help him when the day came and he might have to stand trial. He kept a record of our names for years, and indeed, when Czerwinski came to trial in Germany in 1979, I received a letter from his lawyer in the mail, calling on me to testify in his defense.

Yes, incredible. More than 30 years after the war ended, a letter arrived at my home in Ramat Gan, Israel, from a German lawyer asking me to come and testify for the defense at the trial of this ruthless Nazi killer. They offered me plane tickets to Germany and to cover all my expenses.

I never bothered to answer the letter. When a German police officer sent by the prosecution came to Israel, I gave him my testimony, telling him of our experiences in a camp controlled by the ruthless murderer. I am not sure this was the testimony Czerwinski was hoping for…

I had no idea how the trial ended. I called the Israeli police officer who had accompanied the prosecution investigators, but he insisted he did not know and that there were no results as of yet. At that point, I decided to let it go. I preferred to focus on my life in the present rather than the past.

Research, which was done for this book, provided me with the information. I learned that the trial had gone on for 13 years, in several stages. It began in January 1978 and three and a half years later, in August 1981, was stopped due to Czerwinski having a heart attack. The law required continuity of the legal process and subsequently all 200 testimonies given during the trial, including my own, lost their legal validity over the years.

Czerwinski continued living in Germany, near the city of Hanover. He worked - not ironically - as a butcher. In 1985, he was again arrested, based on new evidence revealed to committees by his deputy, Joseph Schmidt. Schmidt had agreed to testify against Czerwinski in exchange for immunity for his part in the crimes committed in Lagischa. The trial was renewed but dragged on for a long time because of Czerwinski's medical condition. It concluded only in 1989, when the former camp commander was 66 years old. With the aid of testimony by a Jewish prisoner at Lagischa – Abraham Schechter from Israel - Czerwinski was convicted for killing two inmates in 1944. He was sentenced to prison for the rest of his life.

The truth is, although justice had finally been served and the camp commander was punished at the end of his life, this information gave me no satisfaction. Czerwinski had been free for more than forty years after the war. All those years he lived and worked and did not pay for his atrocious crimes. In the end he received a life sentence justice, but for me it had come too little and too late.

Lagischa had taken the lives of many prisoners. There is ample evidence to describe the extraordinary brutality with which the SS guards in the camp treated us. They ill-treated us every day, hour by hour, just because they had the capacity to do so... They starved us, worked us beyond our strengths, and beat us with clubs, rifles, and any weapon at their disposal routinely. For no reason, they abused us in various and creative ways. Today, adjacent to the main gate of the Lagischa power plant, there is a monument in the memory of the camp's victims.

The summer was over. We arrived at Lagischa at the end of May, and at the end of August, they held a selection at the camp before its closure, which was probably coming due to the advance of the Red Army. We were on the field with about 150 'Muselmenn'. (Muselmenn was a slang term used by Jewish prisoners of German Nazi concentration camps during the Holocaust to describe prisoners suffering from a severe combination of starvation and exhaustion, as well as those who had resigned themselves to their impending deaths). It was not clear what our fate would be.

Schreiber, one of the Hungarian commanders, a handsome young man from Budapest, called out to Shoni and me – "You boys, come here to me."

We approached apprehensively. As I have said, any breach of routine in the camp involved great risk.

Schreiber asked if we wanted to leave Lagischa. My eyes met the eyes of my good friend Shani. The same question was in his eyes as well. We did not know what to answer. Shani said quietly, "You only die once." We decided to answer in the affirmative and he told us to prepare our belongings in our bunks. We had nothing to prepare...

The next day they read out a list of numbers and we were both on it. They loaded us on trucks, to where we did not know.

During the trip, there was silence.

After a short time, the truck stopped. They ordered us to get off quickly.

When I saw the gate of an unfamiliar camp, I breathed a sigh of relief. They had not sent us to Birkenau.

We had reached our new 'home,' the main and largest labor camp, Monowitz-Buna - Auschwitz 3.

The rest of the prisoners we were with at the selection in Lagischa were all sent for extermination a short while later, when the camp closed.

By choosing to leave, Shani and I had survived...

Photo of the Lagischa Camp

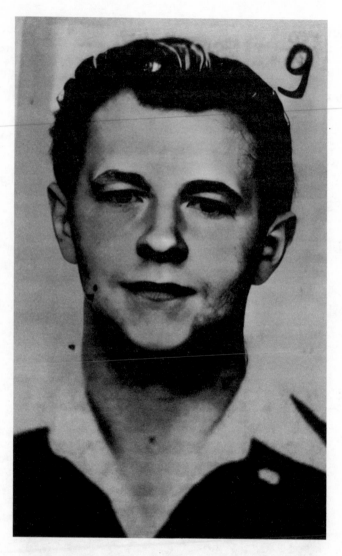

The SS commander of Lagischa camp, Horst Czerwinski.

Auschwitz 3

Buna-Monowitz

Auschwitz 3, known as Buna-Monowitz, was a large camp about eight kilometers from Auschwitz 1. The camp was set up in 1942 in the heart of a huge array of German factories in order to provide forced laborers to construct the Buna-Werka industrial center. As a result, the prisoners called the camp 'Buna.'

Buna was a crowded camp with about 10,000-12,000 prisoners, although it was designated to hold 7000-8000 people. Most of the inmates of the camp were Jews from all parts of Europe. There was also a small number of German and Polish criminals and Polish political prisoners, who lived in a separate compound. We had no contact with them.

As soon as we entered the camp, we were rushed directly to the shower area and told to undress. They gave us soap and a special disinfectant. Armed SS guards led us to a large room where a system of pipes on the ceiling were connected to shower heads.

We were gripped with terror.

By now, we understood very well how the diabolical deception system created by the Germans worked. We knew that there were gas chambers in other camps besides Birkenau.

I continued walking into the large room. There was no other choice. SS officers encircled us on all sides. My heart pounded furiously. The fact that the showerheads were connected to the ceiling was not reassuring. Even in the gas chambers, the Germans set up a standard shower set, to prevent panic and simplify the extermination process.

We looked up in apprehension. No one spoke.

It is hard to describe in words the relief we all felt when jets of water burst from the showerheads above us.

Despite the many diseases that raged in the barracks, the Germans tried to keep the exterior of the camps clean and therefore every passage between the camps primarily included a shower and a sanitization process. Because Buna was a big and crowded camp, the Germans often forced us to go through a sterilization process and I remember these specific showers mainly due to the powder that they scattered all over our bodies. The antiseptic itched and irritated our skin.

After each shower, we would go out naked and wet, and run quickly to the living quarters, where our clothes were. The weather was getting colder and by December, it was freezing. They did not give us towels and the cold air on our wet bodies brought on outbreaks of pneumonia, which was a highly contagious, deadly disease in those days. It claimed many victims.

Sundays in all the Auschwitz camps were days off from work, and every Sunday we would go through the nightmare of hair removal with scissors, dull razors and various hair clippers. They made sure to remove all the hair from our heads, face and entire body. When the 'rest day' was over, they had us line up to present our "Auschwitz Shaves."

The Germans were highly focused on cleanliness in the camp. To an outsider the camp appeared clean and hygienic. The narrow streets between the blocks were well maintained. Although the ground was muddy, there were prisoners assigned to clean it regularly. The blocks that were scattered throughout the camp had a painted wooden exterior and looked presentable. Our living areas inside the block would be cleaned every morning, and the floor was swept and washed. The beds were built on three tiers and were well arranged. We had to stretch the blankets tight every morning, which created the visual illusion of cleanliness.

It was all an illusion. The blocks were overcrowded and two or more people had to sleep on each narrow berth. There were no mattresses and the sleeping surface consisted of sawdust sacks that created dust from prolonged use. They never changed our blankets and they were disinfected only in special situations. Most of them were torn and worn through. The wooden boards of the bunks were inundated with thousands of fleas and bugs that made sleep very difficult at night. Cleaning the rooms every three or four months did nothing to help.

The lice were another enemy against which we fought a bitter war. The Germans were afraid of spreading typhus throughout the camp, which is transmitted by lice. They tested us frequently and we did our best to prevent infection. Luckily, I was able to avoid the disease.

As we had arrived at the camp at the end of August, they gave us the Buna summer uniforms: a shirt that served as a jacket, striped trousers made from thin cloth, a tank top and a hat. We changed clothes every few weeks and repaired them countless times. Along with the uniform, we also received shoes with wooden soles that had no correlation to our foot size. Sometimes they were two different size shoes, in the worst condition imaginable. They had been 'harvested' from the confiscated belongings of Jews. The soles were made of hard wood and were not even suitable for a short walk so we regularly had abrasions and sores on our feet. In the first place, they were worn out, and secondly, they did not give us laces to tie them. We improvised with thin strands of iron wire. We did the same to replace buttons that had fallen off.

The clothes were so worn they were merely rags. Veteran inmates who received socks and underwear said that many of them had been sewn out of tallits, Jewish prayer shawls that were found in the suitcases of the camp inmates. They used them of course to humiliate and mock the sanctity of the tallit for Jews.

At the end of October, the prisoners' uniforms were exchanged for ones from thicker cloth, and old, worn sweaters and jackets taken from the Jewish suitcases were distributed. Unfortunately, in the fall of 1944, at the period when we were incarcerated in Buna, no distribution of winter clothing was made because the warmer uniforms were completely worn out and unsuitable for use. We had to remain with the summer uniforms even during the freezing cold winter. Only a few inmates managed to provide themselves with a slightly warmer sweater or jacket.

Hunger and its consequences were an everyday enemy. Our meals were far from satisfying the body's minimal needs and without protein and vitamins, we became greatly weakened. Bread was the main food that satiated our hunger a little. The fact that there were visible bits of sawdust baked into it did not stop us from quickly swallowing the portion we were given. On some days, we also got a small speck of margarine for the bread. At noon, they distributed thin soup without any seasoning, and in the evening another portion of soup, which included a little potato. In the mornings, we got some coffee-like water. The water in the camp was not drinkable, including the water that came out of the showers.

Prisoners ate potato peels, raw cabbage leaves, beets and rotten potatoes collected out of the kitchen garbage. We were hungry and thirsty all the time.

Camp procedures were harsh and strictly enforced. A day in the life of a prisoner consisted of a long series of duties and carrying out orders. Some were known in advance and some orders came unexpectedly from above, sometimes because of a violent, arbitrary rage of the camp commander.

Our routine included waking up at dawn, standing in the morning lineup, working long hours of hard labor, then the afternoon queue, and the in line for dinner, and going back to the barracks for inspection. Here, too, there was a prisoner in charge of each hut, in most cases a Jewish prisoner. The rest of the guards were German SS.

The camp bell ruled our lives.

It clanged every morning to get us up, informed us of meal times, called us to the various lineups and for any unusual event, and in the evening, it determined when we went to bed. Like herds of cows in a meadow, the ringing of a bell governed our lives. There was nothing personal or humane about our treatment. They summoned us, ordered us, and prepared us; our struggle for survival was passive and silent. Nothing physical was under our control. The Germans determined when we would arise, when we would eat, when we would work or take a shower. They even told us when we could use the toilets without any privacy or consideration for personal and biological needs. The only thing we had control over was our spirits - the capacity to believe that a better future was ahead, while also knowing that there was a high probability we would not live to see it.

The work in the camp was hard labor and our poor physical condition and skills were not up to it.

They divided the prisoners into different command units, which also determined where they were housed. Shani and I were in the "Cable Commando," whose job was digging trenches, and it was very strenuous physical work. The inmates at the site warned us that we would not be able to stand it for long. After months of constant hunger, we were already very thin and weak, and we decided to take a risk. We decided to ask Drucker, the head secretary, for a transfer to a less back-breaking job. At the end of the workday, we approached him in tears, explaining that we did not have the strength to dig. Luckily for us, Drucker spared our lives and said he would try to arrange for a transfer to another, easier assignment. He made it clear that he would not be able to keep the two of us together and that we would have to split up. We agreed.

Already that same evening they called our numbers in the lineup and assigned each of us to a new job. Accordingly, I had to move to a different housing block, next to the one where Shani was.

They put me to work in a factory not far from the camp, where they fashioned devices using mercury. I had to assemble scale parts, working directly with toxic substances and mercury among them. They provided no protective equipment, and as protection against toxins, they told us to be careful not to open our mouths while working. This instruction raised my level of anxiety, but I had no choice. The factory also employed German citizens, who treated us more humanely than the guards.

Each morning we would line up in threes near the camp gate. The SS guards would pass among us and record the numbers of the prisoners before they left for work every day and immediately upon their return.

An orchestra made up of prisoners like ourselves played rhythmic marches when we left the gate in the mornings and returned to the camp every evening. It was one of the most insane things about planet Auschwitz. Stirring music was so far removed from this horrible place, and the sounds of musical instruments where death, hunger and fear reigned supreme was particularly cynical. The orchestra accompanied our departure from the camp and our entry into it and we were forced to march in fives and in rhythm: left-right, left-right...

The factory where I worked was about seven kilometers distance. At the end of the arduous working day, when we no longer had the strength even to stand on our own two feet, we would walk back to camp. As was the custom in all the Auschwitz camps, they held the evening parade as soon as we returned. Here, too, we had to stand in line, motionless for about an hour and sometimes up to three hours. The lineups inflicted greater suffering as winter approached.

Buna was a huge camp and to prevent any breach of discipline, they imposed strict rules and enforced them with extraordinary severity and cruelty. There were gallows spread around the parade ground and almost every morning we were met with the grisly sight of prisoners who had been hanged after trying to escape, or had been caught smuggling, or stealing, or for any reason that popped into the heads of the SS guards. Sometimes they hung them for no particular reason; simply to frighten the rest of us. Part of the hanging ceremony was marching all the prisoners around the gallows – like an Independence Day parade – for a close look at the prisoner who had been hanged. In this horrible way, the Germans maintained constant discipline and immediate and absolute obedience.

It is hard for me to describe the effect these experiences and sights had on the tender soul of a young boy, who grew up in a warm and loving home, free from any hardship or pain. When my grandfather died, they made sure to keep us children away, but now there was no protective armor to separate us - the living - from the many dead we witnessed around us every day. The same imperviousness that we adapted as an instinct that protected us from painful focus on the fate of family members, kept me sane in light of the horrific things I was exposed to at such an early age.

Only four months had passed since we left the ghetto. A short time in ordinary life, and an eternity at Auschwitz, where we faced daily existential danger. Death lay in wait at every corner and our lives were worth less than a clove of garlic. Every day, we struggled for the privilege of staying alive.

As in all the Auschwitz camps, from time to time they held a selection in Buna. Anyone that did not look fit was immediately sent to the Birkenau gas chambers.

When the bell rang announcing a selection, we had to take off all our clothes and stand naked inside our huts. We then had to wait for our number to be called and then go before a group of SS men who had come to the camp specifically for the selection. In the center of the camp stood a lean-to where they sent the naked prisoners who had not successfully passed the selection. At night, SS men accompanied by dogs came and took them away to Birkenau.

In each selection, they sent several hundred inmates to this dreaded shack.

The veteran prisoners and block commanders advised us to exercise before the selection began so that our pale faces would have a little color. They also said we should move quickly and not look at the SS men.

We had very little control in this terrible situation, but we also had occasions where we could make a decision that saved our lives.

The first time my life was saved by a decision I made in a split second was in Birkenau, when I said goodbye to my mother in the selection line. The second time was in the first few weeks of my arrival at Buna.

One day in September, we stood for a long time in the lineup. Though it was the beginning of autumn, it was an unusually hot day. I felt I could no longer stand on my feet. My friends helped me sit down and it turned out I had a fever. I developed an infection from a rash on my foot, and was unable to go to work. There was a hospital unit in the camp but we all knew that going there was dangerous, and there was usually no exit once you entered. Despite the risk, I had no choice. The devoted friends around me saw my condition and realized that I needed immediate treatment.

They took me to the hospital. The medical staff were prisoners themselves, Jewish doctors who spoke mostly Polish and/or German. They had nurse assistants who had no medical background and knew nothing about sterility maintenance or medical procedures. The medicine cabinet in the clinic contained mainly medicines taken from suitcases of prisoners who had arrived in Auschwitz and they were not always still effective for use.

I was there overnight. The next morning I felt better, but I was very weak and still had a fever. One of the doctors approached me and warned me to get out of there before the next selection. I was barely able to get to my feet but I determined that there was nothing to do but to return to my barracks. Fortunately, I recovered relatively quickly and remained fit for work.

In the autumn of 1944, the Allied forces started bombing the area heavily and one of their targets was Buna's industrial factories. We would hear the shelling, and longed for the day when the war would end and our living nightmare would be over.

The shelling of the factories caused severe damage, and disrupted the normal work routine. Renovations to the factories were needed. To my joy, the Germans looked for young prisoners who could work on the repairs, and after a few weeks in the mercury factory, I was transferred to a school for training in construction.

Among the inmates in the camp were professionals in almost every field, who taught us skills in every field in which we were employed. Training in construction lasted about two weeks, during which I learned how to construct walls, make cement and perform basic building work. They sent me to work in Buna's industrial area at sites that had been bombed and damaged. The Germans put barrels near the factories and during the shelling; these barrels released thick smoke to obscure the location of the factories and to make sure the planes could not pinpoint them. The Americans knew that a huge industrial area was spread around Buna and rained down shells indiscriminately. The planes came in waves, filling the sky.

When the first alarms sounded we were ordered to run to a nearby underground shelter. During the first shelling I did that, but the shelling caused the shelter to sway like a ship on the sea. The walls shook violently and we were sure we would not make it out of there alive. It was so frightening that some of the prisoners, myself included, decided it was better to run to the open fields and not go into the shelters.

From then on, whenever we heard the alarm we lay down in the open fields, hugging the ground. Although we were exposed without any protection from the shelling, we felt much better. From where we were lying we could look up and see above us hundreds of high-altitude silver "birds," dropping huge amounts of bombs covering a wide area. We could easily identify the American bombers that were flying at an altitude high above the German planes. I felt a certain comfort seeing the destruction the planes made in the industrial areas. We all hoped in our hearts that the pilots were launching some of their deadly cargo on the crematoria of Birkenau.

It is possible that as you read these lines you may ask why did we not take advantage of the chaos during the shelling and run. We were in an open field, outside the camp fence. Why did we not think of taking advantage of the opportunity created by the shelling and escape?

The truth is we were scared. We knew that any deviation from the Germans' instructions meant immediate death. We saw examples of this every day. Also, where would we go? Wearing ragged striped uniforms, with shaved heads and a tattooed number on our arms - any passerby would easily identify us as Jewish camp prisoners. I was a young boy, in a foreign land, and I was frightened. I hoped - and by this point I already believed - that the end of the war was near and I wanted to survive. The instinct for life was greater than the instinct for freedom. Attempting to escape was risking your life and almost certain death.

The Germans succeeded in neutralizing the innate desire for independence in the human psyche and they extinguished within us the urge to take action and fight for freedom and liberty. The instinct we developed was a passive one, and our struggle was basically to keep our bodies and souls alive. Looking back it is clear to me that we actually did fight for our survival in what we did. We understood that the best odds for staying alive and perhaps gaining our freedom in the future was not through active struggle.

Escape did not at any stage seem to me to be a viable option and I did not see any hope of gaining my immediate freedom by trying to escape.

The shelling went on almost daily. Buna was a large factory site and the Americans aimed to inflict a lethal blow on German industry in order to damage it as much as possible. As early as 1944, the Allies knew what was really going on behind the fences of the Nazi camps. When aerial photographs of Auschwitz became available and there were testimonies of escaped prisoners about what was happening inside the camps, Churchill ordered the shelling of the camps themselves. His order was never carried out. Jewish leaders were pleading with the American and British governments to send bombers to Birkenau or bomb the tracks that were used to transfer hundreds of thousands of Hungarian Jews in the early summer of 1944.

The fate of the Jews was not a major concern for the United States, Britain, or their allies in its waging of the war. Just a few miles from where they were bombing on a regular basis, the killing factories churned on uninterrupted. To this day I do not understand why the planes did not bomb Birkenau. This is one of the greatest stains on the Allies' conduct during the Nazi campaign of genocide of the Jews the Holocaust.

The Germans and their collaborators continued to slaughter us unimpeded, while those who could have stopped or reduced the mass killing by bombing the tracks or the gas chambers directly did nothing.

Only in November 1944 did the Germans stop operating the extermination apparatus in Birkenau, because the Russian army was approaching and evidence of the atrocities that took place in the camp had to be destroyed.

In October 1944, they held the last selection at Buna, following which the Birkenau gas chambers were dismantled because the Russians were advancing from the east and the Nazis wanted to destroy evidence of the atrocities they carried out there. In this final selection, they sent 850 victims for extermination.

It is clear to any reasonable person that a single bombing to stop the relentless movement of trains towards the gas chambers in Birkenau or damage to the crematoria would have saved tens and possibly hundreds of thousands of Jewish lives.

The question of why this did not happen is an enigma to this day...

Autumn, 1944.

I turned fourteen in September.

I did not even remember it was my birthday. I had no awareness of the date or its meaning.

A year had passed since my bar mitzvah. One year - an eternity.

The Tishrei holidays passed us by. A new year of the Hebrew calendar began, without a prayer or the blowing of the shofar for the first time in my life.

Yom Kippur, the holiest day of the year in the Hebrew calendar, was just another day in Auschwitz. The apathy and our daily struggle for survival disrupted the centuries-old connection to the tradition from which we came. The struggle for survival in the camps was accompanied by an almost total disconnect from the past, even in the religious sense. Our detachment from the dimension of time, and the practical difficulty of keeping a tradition without a tallit, Tefillin, and communal prayer services all contributed to this indifference.

In addition, many of us had lost faith. God was not with us there, and I believe that a great many of the camp inmates found themselves in a particularly severe spiritual crisis, when not only was their physical world shattered, but also their belief in religion.

Was that why we were the Chosen People? Chosen to be gassed, starved to death, and die from deadly disease?

Eli Wiesel, who was also at Buna at that time though we did not know it then, aptly described the conflict in the hearts of many Jews, between tradition and religious belief and the sense that God had abandoned them. In his book "Night" Wiesel describes his feelings in the face of the cremations he witnessed on the day he arrived in Birkenau: "Why must I sanctify His name? The Lord God,

King of the world, All Powerful God…Is silent. Why should I acknowledge Him?"

Winter, 1944.

We heard the echoes of the approaching cannons and realized that the Russian front was getting nearer. Snow fell, blanketing the camp in white. Our barracks windows were permanently covered over with a shell of thin frost. A new enemy played a major role in our efforts to survive - the freezing cold. We were not adequately dressed and we shivered almost all the time.

One day the bell rang in the afternoon, calling the block leaders to the camp commander. They came back from the meeting and told us that they were going to evacuate the camp and we would be transferred to camps in Germany.

During the months I was in Buna there were occasional rumors that the war was coming to an end. This time we sensed that the rumors were true. We knew we had to do everything we could to survive until then.

The organization for evacuation began. They distributed rations for the journey: double servings of bread and margarine.

The Auschwitz era had ended.

405,000 inmates went through registration as inmates in the Auschwitz camps. Of course, this number does not include those who were sent directly for extermination.

Of the 405,000 about 65,000 had so far survived.

In its years of operation, approximately 1,500,000 men, women and children were murdered at Auschwitz, representing about one out of four of all Jews murdered in the Holocaust.

In mid-January 1945, the Germans quickly dismantled the camps.

Today only twenty percent of the original structures remain. Auschwitz 1 consisted mainly of stone buildings and they were mostly preserved. In Birkenau only a relatively small number of the buildings remained. The residents of the area dismantled the wooden barracks immediately after the camp was evacuated and used them for heating fuel.

On January 27, 1945, the Red Army was nearing the gates of Auschwitz.

The Death Marches

At the end of December 1944, an order was issued to evacuate all prisoners of war and inmates of the concentration camps and transfer them to Germany, to places where their labor force could continue to be exploited.

Despite the certain imminent defeat of Nazi Germany, the instructions from Berlin were clear: the mass extermination was to continue through death marches, famine, and the spread of disease. Any survivors would be relocated in Germany, for further forced labor in the service of the German army and German industry.

About 58,000 prisoners were evacuated and on January 21, the evacuation of all the camps in the area ended.

On January 27, 1944, 6 days after the last prisoners had left the camp, the Red Army entered the gates of Auschwitz. The Russian soldiers were stunned to discover neat piles of men's and women's clothing, mountains of shoes, glasses, and huge sacks of human hair packed and ready for shipment to Germany.

The horrors began unfolding. From this moment, the world would no longer be able to ignore the existence of barely alive human skeletons in striped clothes, and the gruesome stories they had to tell...

The evacuation of the Buna camp began on January 17, 1945. The Germans dragged 11,000 inmates of the camp on a 70-kilometer march.

The nightmare started one evening, when my block was called to the parade square, the Appellplatz.

They distributed a larger portion of bread that would be enough for the next few days. It was uncertain when we would eat again and I carefully guarded the little food I had received.

I wore a plain shirt and thin, ragged pants. I was wearing shoes but no socks. That is how I set off. Shani was not with me; the Germans evacuated the blocks according to the command units in which we worked. I looked around for him but it was impossible to spot anyone in the horde of inmates.

I was alone. They did not give us any time to organize ourselves. SS soldiers encircled us, shouting orders.

We stood at the gate in threes, ready to move. They made it clear to us that they would shoot anyone who disobeyed the directives.

Darkness began to envelop the camp. Snow fell relentlessly. We were freezing, exhausted, and weak.

We left the camp gate and turned left towards the dark road, marching at a fast pace in threes. All around us were SS soldiers armed and ready to fire.

Anyone who stopped, they shot immediately. At one point, the shootings stopped, but the cold and snow were no less effective in eliminating stragglers.

We tried to keep up the fast pace dictated by the SS soldiers with their cursing and shouting. Cigarette butts were seen strewn on the road, and here and there a morsel of fruit that had been thrown away. People around me quickly bent down and picked up anything thrown on the road that seemed edible. As I was marching, I spotted some apple scraps thrown to the ground. I quickly picked up the remainder of the fruit and thrust it into my mouth. I had almost forgotten what an apple tasted like.

We did not know where we were going or when we would stop. When would they let us rest? Our legs moved mechanically.

We passed the factory area and after about 7 or 8 kilometers of marching, we turned left again.

We came upon a road sign: "Auschwitz" and turned in the opposite direction.

It went like that for hours on end, in the night. Our eyes closed but our bodies kept going. It was as if we had an engine inside of us, and knew that once we lay down it could not be restarted to keep us among the living.

These marches were aptly labelled "death marches" because anyone who did not march died on the spot. Thousands of prisoners who had survived the horrors of the camp for months perished on the roads; their strength failed them and they collapsed on the sides of the road. They were either instantly shot or froze to death. In the area of our march, winter temperatures that freezing winter of 1945 dipped to minus twenty-five degrees Celsius. The days were short and the sun set early, so we did most of the walking in the dark at extremely low temperatures. To this must be added the lack of a nutritious diet or warm clothes, physical exhaustion, and the sheer exertion needed to walk tens of miles- a difficult task even for healthy and fit people.

The roads were covered with snow. German army vehicles retreating from the front often passed us and we had to make room for them and walk much of the time on the edge of the roads, where the snow piled up in high drifts. The march became more and more difficult, but we had to keep up with the pace dictated by the SS soldiers. Along the way, we saw countless dead bodies frozen stiff on the side of the road. The sight was appalling. Indifference and the numbing of our senses was the only way we could go on: to harden our hearts and neutralize our feelings in the face of these dreadful sights.

The wind whipped us mercilessly. I could not feel my feet. My whole body suffered terribly from the bitter cold, which penetrated sharply through the thin cloth shirt I was wearing. The temperature was about twenty degrees below zero. It is hard to imagine survival in such conditions without socks or a warm coat.

Night turned into day. We kept marching - parched, hungry, and gasping for breath.

Many around me fell into the snow, stopped to rest for a moment, just gave up, or ran out of strength.

Our thirst was intense but luckily, the snow that fell non-stop gave us drink.

There was a great temptation to stop and end the nightmare. To this day, I do not know how to explain how I endured it and managed to keep walking for so many hours.

By nightfall, we arrived at an abandoned factory and finally got permission to stop. We hurried to grab a corner to spend the night relatively comfortably. Everywhere, people lay exhausted and breathing heavily. It was hard to find a vacant spot. Many of the exhausted prisoners did not wake up when the next morning came.

We continued to march. We still did not know where we were being led, but at this point, we were already used to the uncertainty that ruled our lives. At night, we arrived at the Gleiwitz concentration camp, which was near a train station. The camp was in a state of collapse and there was commotion everywhere. I looked for a place to rest.

I cannot describe the immense joy and relief that came over me when I found my good friend, Shani, among the prisoners in the camp. We were together again.

We settled into a warehouse with a pile of clothing, glad to lay down our weary bodies for a dreamless night's sleep. We spent several nights at Gleiwitz, under the strict surveillance of the SS soldiers, with no food or drink. We could hear the approaching Russian army cannon fire almost non-stop.

We awaited the instructions of the SS officers for our next evacuation orders to an unknown destination.

One of the mornings, we wandered hungrily around the deserted camp, scouring the ground for any scraps of food.

The camp was completely empty, but in one of the barracks, which apparently had served the camp guards, Shani saw an inverted nightstand lying on the floor. When we turned it over, we found packets of chicory powder inside, which was used to make a coffee substitute. Chicory is a fleshy plant that grows in nature, and it was possible to make a drink from it that tasted a bit like coffee in the absence of the real thing. Shani quickly filled his pockets with the powder.

"What do you need it for?" I asked him.

Without any other food, we ate the powder dry for seven days. We shared it equally, a spoon for me and a spoon for him.

One morning they called us with shouting to assemble and they prodded us to walk quickly to a nearby train depot.

They did not let us sit. We stood and waited for a train to come that would take us into the unknown. Towards evening, there was a rattling sound on the tracks, and soon, a train with a long line of open freight cars about 1.2 meters high stopped near us. It was a train intended for transporting cattle. Inside the exposed carriages was a great deal of snow that had accumulated on the floors. An advantage of the open cars was that the air was not stifling, but it was also freezing cold, and we had no protection from it.

There was a rumor that they were taking us to Germany, but no one knew for certain where our final destination was. In the uncertainty all around us, we took comfort in being together again.

Shani looked at me and said, "Moishie, I'll beat you if you leave me and disappear."

I had no such intention.

They told us to get on the train and take a seat, but it was impossible to sit with such a dense pack of bodies, so we stood, crammed like sardines and frozen to a degree that is hard to describe. This is how the train journey started.

Many did not survive and we piled the dead in the corner of the car. As their number increased, we were able to create enough space where it was possible to get down on our knees and give our feet a rest. It had been four days since they had given us any food.

We continued under these conditions for the next few days.

Imagine to yourselves...

A slowly rolling cattle train on its way to an unknown destination.

It was January, the height of winter. Terrible cold. The wind whipped inside the cars, lowering the temperature even further. There was nowhere to take shelter, nothing to eat. We sat freezing, thinly dressed and without socks. The temptation to close one's eyes and sink into eternity was especially powerful and some people around me fell asleep and awoke no more...

Snow fell continuously on the first day of the journey, providing us drink and allowing us survive, but the icy snow also took its toll. More than half of the inmates in the car froze to death.

I was 14 years and 4 months old.

At this age, in normal times, adults protect young people. Even when we encounter death, there is usually no visual exposure. Despite my young age, by January 1945 I was hardened by it. In the nine months since I climbed with Mom and Arnold aboard the freight train that took us to Poland, I had to deal with the harsh and cruel sight of the dead.

We had become indifferent to almost everything except the will to live. Those among us who had become indifferent even to life gave up and perished.

Shani and I tried to position ourselves on one side of the car so we could lean against it and rest. Next to us, we recognized a boy our age from Bergsas named Alberger. He had managed to survive the camp with his father. His father warned us throughout the trip not to fall asleep and pleaded with us to persevere. "Eat the snow and hold on; whoever falls asleep freezes to death," he repeated to us.

I do not know how I was able to keep going, when so many others broke down and closed their eyes forever. I remember setting one goal only: to keep awake, to keep breathing.

After the first day of travel, the snow stopped falling.

Without snow, our thirst became almost unbearable. At one of the stops, I felt I could no longer do without drinking something. They allowed us to get down for a short time and I decided to approach one of the soldiers. Risking my life, I asked him to fill a container of hot water for us from water that had leaked from the boilers near the train's locomotive. I told Shani that I did not think he would kill us, but even if he did, our lives were no longer much value anyway. Fortunately, the soldier agreed. The water he brought us saved us.

The train continued traveling on. From time to time, we stopped at a station but they did not allow us to get off the car again. At one of the stations where the train stopped for a supply of coal, we came across a convoy of soldiers, who were retreating from the front. Their train had stopped on a parallel track. They threw us some food.

The trip lasted about five days.

The train traveled slowly and stopped often. There was no longer a problem of crowding in the car; there was a sense of death all around.

Outside, the landscape had changed. It looked like it was from another reality. Cities, whole buildings, with no sign of shelling.

We had arrived in Germany. We finally stopped at a station with the name "Weimar" above it. We waited in the cars while they detached several of the train cars and some of the prisoners continued in another direction. After the split, we continued on our way.

In a few miles, we reached our final destination, the Buchenwald concentration camp.

Open evacuation cars from Geilvitz to Buchenwald

Buchenwald

The train stopped.

Again, shouts of "Schnell!" – "Fast!"

Again, SS guards, terrifying dogs, snarling and baring their teeth.

And again, the fences.

Buchenwald.

The Nazis established the camp in 1937, in the heart of a vast forest in the eastern section of Germany near the historic city of Weimar, the cradle of German culture. The concentration camp is a ten-minute drive from the Weimar National Theater. Its purpose was the imprisonment of opponents of the Nazi regime and the Communists, who were classified as enemies.

The first prisoners in Buchenwald were members of the Communist Party of Germany, who organized an extensive underground movement in the camp. Then came various others who were considered threats by the Nazi regime.

During the war, Buchenwald housed prisoners from dozens of nations, including several future European leaders:

one prisoner was Dr. Konrad Adenauer, an anti-Nazi who was mayor of Cologne. After the war, he would become West Germany's first Chancellor. Prisoner Leon Blum later became Prime Minister of France. The mayor of Prague, Petr Zenkl, was also among the Buchenwald prisoners.

At a later stage, Jewish prisoners, mostly Poles, were transferred to Buchenwald, and a few of them joined the underground, which in 1943 created the "International Camp Committee" (ICC). The underground was the only connection between the Jewish and the political prisoners. The Jews were quarantined in a separate area of the camp, located in marshlands called the "Little Camp." They were "offered" much harsher conditions than those of political prisoners, some of whom were appointed to oversight and management positions in the Jewish blocs. This fact was widely criticized after the war, as it involved some adherence to German policy. In many camps, the guards were cruel and abused the Jews, making their lives more miserable and their living conditions worse.

In Buchenwald, some political prisoners in positions of oversight were able to use their status to save lives.

In January 1945, with the evacuation of the Auschwitz camps, several hundred children and adolescents aged six to sixteen arrived in Buchenwald.

I was among them.

We got off the train. It was noon.

Only those who could stand could get out of the caravan. Some had no strength left and remained sitting on the train, amid the piles of the dead. Out of approximately one hundred people who boarded the car - only a few survived.

We had no idea what the place was. We encountered veteran prisoners in uniforms similar to ours, and armed SS soldiers. The main concern of any move to a new place was the fear they were going to gas us, using the same methods we knew from Auschwitz.

We advanced on foot towards the camp, which was surrounded by high barbed wire fences.

An inscription in German stood out on the entrance gate – "JEDEM DAS SEINE": "Every man to his own fate."

These words cynically and frighteningly reflected what was going on inside the gates, not only in Buchenwald but also in all the camps.

Our former lives, before we were expelled from our homes, had taught us mutual support, concern for others, and acceding to another. We had a vision of the interrelationship among human beings, and the strength of community and togetherness. We grew up on the precepts of the Torah, and the concept that all Israel are as one, intertwined with each other.

Some of us lost the battle to maintain this tradition. For many of the camp inmates the rules of love for others and mutual concern had disappeared as useless baggage. Here the rules were different. The Holocaust taught us that indeed, each man has his own destiny.

This sentence reflected the new worldview we had to develop which meant, among other things, a certain indifference towards the suffering of others and a focus solely on our capacity to survive. It may sound cruel but it was merely an intuitive numbness we adopted in our struggle to stay alive and sane.

In the camps, every slice of bread, every tablespoon of soup meant a better chance of enduring.

Many of those around us, who had believed in friendship and mutual support in our previous lives, now stole from each other, without feeling guilt or pangs of conscience. I ate my portion of bread in small pieces, and kept the leftover bits under my head while I slept. Shani still tearfully remembers when a portion of bread was stolen from him.

Part of the loss of our humanity was also a loss of values. The Germans had managed to get many of us to act like animals and not as human beings in the struggle for survival.

Yet, even within this world of shattered values, there were also many instances of mutual concern, sacrifice, and giving up for the sake of the other.

We advanced into the camp. The SS soldiers hurried us along with curses and beatings.

We stopped at the parade square, which was at the center of every Nazi camp. We lined up in fives and they told us to throw all our personal belongings on a pile in the middle of the field. The Germans burned all the meager belongings of the 'new' prisoners to attempt to prevent the transmission of disease.

They led us to a huge room and ordered us to strip naked. We threw our clothes into a pile and they took them away. They told us that we had to take a shower and go through a disinfection process, as part of the camp absorption process.

We moved to the shower hall, again in silence.

We stood naked and waited. We knew that there was a chance that these were our final moments.

Frozen jets of water burst from the taps.

We did not feel the cold, only the relief that washed over our bodies. Despite the uncertainty of what was to come, we felt happy.

We later learned that a crematorium had been set up in the camp to incinerate the dead, but there was no active mass gassing. The harsh conditions in Buchenwald took care of assuring that tens of thousands of prisoners in Buchenwald would die of exhaustion or disease during the war. The crematorium operated non-stop 24 hours a day.

After showers and disinfection in a chlorine bath, veteran prisoners shaved us from head to toe. They worked in silence and carried out the task mechanically. None of them looked at us or spoke to us. Afterwards, we were sent to the quarantine block for an interim period. The Germans wanted to be certain we had not brought any diseases with us and we were forbidden to go anywhere for about a week.

We ran naked in the iciness of January from the showers to the quarantine block, where new prisoners' uniforms awaited us, identical in design to those we wore in Buna, including the wooden shoes. The difference was in the numbering method, which was different from that used in Auschwitz. They gave each of us a new number, which was sewn onto the striped shirt we wore.

From now on, I am prisoner 121207.

A symbol was added to the prisoner number, intended to divide the camp inmates according to their nationality.

A yellow triangle was the symbol for the Jews. The uniforms of the political prisoners were marked differently. Polish prisoners, for example, had a red triangle after their number.

We did not know this then, but at the end of 1944, when the evacuation of the concentration and extermination camps in Eastern Europe began and the German army was in retreat on all fronts, the leaders of the political underground in Buchenwald made a decision to try to save the children who arrived at the camp. The main supporters of this effort were Antonin Kalina, a Czech-born Christian, and Jack Weber, a Polish-Jewish inmate, both members of the underground.

Kalina and his comrades put pressure on the Germans to place the children in a separate hut within the camp. The Germans preferred to prevent unrest in the camp, so they responded to pressure from Kalina and his friends and agreed to house children aged 12 to 16 in an isolated hut named "Kinder Block 66."

Kalina asked to be put in charge of Block 66, and moved the children and teenagers there from all around the camp.

After some time in the quarantine block, they placed us in the permanent barracks.

Buchenwald was divided into three sections. The main area of the camp was near the entrance gate where the political prisoners were housed and the camp administration and the parade ground were located. In the middle section was the huge quarantine hut and in the lower area was the "Little Camp." At its far end, near the forest, was Block 66.

The veteran inmates told us that youngsters our age should do all they can to get into Block 66.

When they placed us, they transferred me to Block 66, but Shani was not transferred with me. I had mixed feelings. I knew that this block was for youngsters and that it was better for me to move there, but it was hard to leave my friends. Shani promised that he would do everything in his power to join me.

They had split us up. Shani later said that he cried bitterly after I left; he felt that his soul was taken from him when I left and that he was lost. He was sure he would die after saying goodbye to me. Fortunately, one of the German overseers took a liking to him. Shani took advantage of this good relationship and pleaded to be transferred to the children's block.

A few days later, the request was approved and we were together again.

Block 66 was at the lower end camp, near the forest. It was in the middle of a neglected swamp that was a health hazard. An electrified fence separated our block from the main camp. The block housed about 1,000 children. It was run by Antonin Kalina and his assistants: Dr. Fluser, a Czech born Jew, and Gustav Schiller, a Jew from Poland.

Block 66 was crowded. The bunks were 4-5 levels high and so packed that some of us had to sleep on the floor. Despite this, we were glad of our good fortune, as our treatment was significantly better and healthier thanks to the members of the underground who ran the block.

One of the greatest benefits was that they did not send us to work. The older inmates in the camp, aged 17 and over, were made to carry out arduous forced labor. Working conditions were particularly harsh in the January-February cold and many did not survive. The very fact that we were not sent to perform hard physical work greatly eased our situation, which was bad enough in any case.

The only activities they required of us was to report to the morning and evening line-ups. We were left to our own devices the rest of the day. The parades were held in the camp square, which was far from our apartment block. January 1945 was a particularly freezing month, with temperatures hovering around twenty degrees below zero. The parades lasted hours and we were abused, standing out in the cold, thinly dressed, and obliged to wave our hats above our heads and put them back on, repeatedly.

Kalina had a brilliant idea. He told the Germans that typhus was raging in our block and that it would be better for them to make the count themselves inside the block, while committing to updating the Germans every morning and evening. The Germans, who were very much afraid of a typhus epidemic spreading in the camp, accepted his offer. We were allowed to go through the morning and evening counts inside the block. Kalina counted us and allowed us to do as we wished.

This was important because it was freezing cold outside. In addition, to better cope with the extreme cold at night, Kalina made sure that each of us got two blankets.

We spent little time outdoors. Independently walking around the camp was forbidden, and most of the time we spent lying sprawled in the crowded blocks.

The disadvantage of this situation was catching illnesses, which spread easily.

Kalina took care of us in every aspect that was within his authority. Contrary to everything we had known in other camps, we were not beaten, we were treated fairly, and the food was shared equally. Still, we were constantly hungry because even in Buchenwald we got a meal of soup once a day. In the morning and evening, we had to settle for coffee-water.

After the end of the war, we realized how this placement in block 66 had saved our lives. In the other blocks in Buchenwald where Jews were housed, very different conditions prevailed. Every morning several dozen dead bodies of prisoners who could not withstand the cold, hunger, and hard labor were removed from the block.

The months passed by. Winter gave way to the first days of spring. It was March and Passover was approaching. A year had passed since we celebrated in the ghetto, without matzah, without a holiday atmosphere, but together. Here, in Buchenwald, for the first time in my life, I was on my own for the holiday, without my parents or brother. I did not feel any holiday atmosphere.

Keeping the holidays was sacred to us, and from a young age I had attended synagogue with my father every Saturday, and felt a deep connection to Judaism and its commandments.

Since last year, when we were hauled in cattle cars to Auschwitz, my world shattered not only physically but also mentally and emotionally. I had been abandoned to my fate, without any of my family. I had witnessed extreme human cruelty, mass deaths and had endured conditions not fit for animals, let alone human beings.

I spent Rosh Hashanah and Yom Kippur at Buna without knowing what the date was. I had moved away from all the religious and traditional symbols that had accompanied me all my life.

One evening, just before Passover, a group of boys came to me and asked me to pray with them at the back of the block, to make a minyan. For the first time in my life, I did not know how I was going to pray. To whom do I direct my prayers?

What was there left to believe in?

I looked at them with my heart pounding. Since I had left my home, twelve months earlier, I had not prayed.

"How do we pray? What do we pray with? And what sense does it make?" I asked them. I felt that the world of faith, from which we came, had been destroyed. It was not clear if and how it could be rebuilt.

"One of the prisoners, Laser, has a prayer book that he smuggled out of Auschwitz," They told me.

Religious education, which was a central part of my life from the day I was born, was strong and won over my misgivings and I joined them. We held the prayer service according to tradition, hidden within the block.

I remember thinking to myself, "If we ever get out of here alive, who will believe our story, this crazy reality in which we live?"

Years later, I learned that Laser, the boy who smuggled the prayer book out of Auschwitz, was Nobel Peace Prize laureate Eli Wiesel.

I wrote him a personal letter and mentioned that prayer service in Buchenwald, at Passover 1945. The reply I received said that it was indeed him, the boy who gathered us around his prayer book to experience a moment when the flame of Jewish tradition was ignited and not extinguished...

The roar of the shelling came closer and an uncharacteristic sloppiness began in the camp.

On April 4, they stopped taking workers out for morning shifts. It was clear that the end was near.

One day, Kalina entered the block with a particularly serious look on his face. He ordered us to change our shirts with the shirts of political prisoners who had died in the camp that had numbers on them and a red triangle next to them. Under his direction, we ripped the numbers and the yellow emblems from our clothes, and Kalina burned all evidence of our being Jews. The leaders of the underground understood that the Germans were about to reach Block 66 to evacuate all the Jewish prisoners to death marches from Buchenwald to unknown destinations. The aim of the Germans was clear: to leave no trace of the Jews, which would be a living testimony to their evil actions.

Kalina saved us by having us exchange our identities with dead political prisoners.

Changing clothes was just one of the actions the underground took to save our lives. The Germans were very orderly and the camp administration had accurate documentation of each prisoner who came to Buchenwald, his number, and national/ethnic origin. To prevent the Germans from discovering our true identity, the underground set fire to the camp administration offices. The prisoners' folders and their details were destroyed, so that the Germans could not have any record of the Polish dead who were resurrected in our image, nor the Jewish prisoners who had "disappeared" from the camp.

Kalina had to act quickly and without hesitation. The day after we changed shirts, a call was heard throughout the camp for all Jews to gather in the parade ground. Kalina instructed us in an authoritative and determined voice not to obey the SS instructions. When the SS soldiers came to the block and asked all the Jews to leave, we stayed in our places. It was the first time we had disobeyed orders. We all trembled, but Kalina had reassured us and we relied on him. Our block manager and his aide greeted the Germans and said emphatically that there were no Jews left in Block 66. They risked their lives, lying with convincing determination. When the SS soldiers entered the block and found that the prisoners were indeed wearing uniforms with a Polish emblem, they left the area and left us alone.

Kalina saved our lives by his actions. He stood firm in his insistence that there were no Jewish children in the block and thanks to him we remained in the camp, while Jewish prisoners in other blocks were forced on marches, which they did not survive.

It was early spring, in the month of April. The surrounding forests began to bloom and become green after the harsh winter. As the days passed the sounds of shelling intensified, and the soldiers ran around the camp. It became clear there was to be a complete evacuation.

On April 6, an assembly took place in which the camp administration informed us that several blocks would be evacuated every day.

Further, from that day on, no soup or bread would be distributed. Kalina asked that we be evacuated last.

Every day thousands of prisoners left the camp gates. Most of them were found dead by American forces, lying frozen in open train cars into which they were lifted after falling in the snow.

By April 9, about 20,000 people remained in Buchenwald.

During the morning parade, a message was spread that by the end of the day the entire camp would be evacuated, including the children's block, block 66. The Germans were determined to empty the entire camp before the arrival of Allied forces. The plan was to finish the evacuation and blow up the camp, in order to destroy all the evidence of the atrocities that took place there.

The speakers thundered orders which made it clear that everyone had to get out of the block immediately and go up to Appellplatz. When we got to the parade grounds, we saw crowds of people, organized to exit the camp.

The German objective was clear: to march us to death. Even when it was obvious that the end of the war was only a matter of time, the exterminations kept going full speed.

Despite our knowing that we were going on a march that we would probably not survive, there was nothing we could do. The SS raided the camp with intensified searches to see that no one was left behind. We lined up in fives, ready to go.

Suddenly an alarm sounded, followed by a series of loud explosions. The Germans ran around the courtyard of the parades, shouting orders. The SS soldiers hurried to lock the gate and rushed us back to the block. For the past six days, we ate nothing except for a few scraps we found. We returned to the block and lay there all day, hungry and weak.

The shelling continued. At times, alarms sounded throughout the camp and immediately afterwards cannons thundered with a deafening noise. When the shelling ceased, night had already fallen. SS officers informed us that the evacuation would take place the next morning.

On the morning of April 10, orders sounded in the public address system - all prisoners must report to the parade ground again quickly, line up in fives and be ready to move. I looked around me. Block 66 was buzzing with youngsters ages 13-17. Everyone rushed out of the hut.

A thought flashed through my mind.

Our block stood on a hillside, and at its far end, under the window, I had spotted several loose planks. I was hoping that under the block floor there would be a gap resulting from the slope of the hill. I looked out the window and made a decision.

"I am not going out," I announced. "I am staying here. What will be will be!"

I knelt down and managed to detach the planks relatively easily. I quickly got into the small, dark niche. Shani hurried in after me. Fortunately, there was a space between the floor of the hut and the soil of the hill on which it stood. Small and cramped, but room enough for both of us. We crouched down and covered our hiding place with the planks above. The air barely penetrated the small spaces between the wooden boards. We lay, our bodies folded up in the gloom, close together and quiet.

Footsteps and voices came closer. SS soldiers entered the hut and quickly scanned it, searching for more inmates. We held our breath. After a time that seemed like an eternity, we heard their footsteps receding and breathed a sigh of relief.

We were hungry and thirsty, and our bodies ached from the lying down, but we did not dare move. We lost the sense of time - day turned to night, and again day.

We huddled there for more than 24 hours, without food or water, listening for what was going on outside. The noise of the explosions grew louder. Gradually the voices of the German soldiers and all the shouts and the orders faded to silence all around.

Then again, there were shouts, this time in different languages.

My whole body ached from lying motionless, but we were still afraid to go out.

We took short, slow breaths, to try to keep the air from running out.

From the noise outside it was clear that something was going on. Our hiding place was close to the hut window and curiosity overcame our fear. We decided to climb out of the hiding place and crawl over to the window, which was right above us, to see what was going on. We carefully lifted the floor planks above us. Our eyes squinted in the bright light after hours of lying in the dark.

We peeked out the window. Our hut was right at the end of the camp, only about twenty meters from the fence that surrounded Buchenwald, at the edge of the forest. We saw men with weapons, working hard to take down the camp's inner barbed wire fences. Later we understood that these were members of the underground, who were taking over the camp. From a distance, we saw SS soldiers shedding their uniforms in an attempt to impersonate civilians, miraculously entering the forest wearing only their underwear.

We realized that the persecutors had become the persecuted, but we were still afraid to leave the hut. The experience of many months taught us to be extra cautious, and it was nearly impossible to break free from the terror of the SS soldiers.

We went back to our hiding place, our hearts beating with hope.

After what seemed like an eternity, we again heard voices outside the hut. We listened anxiously, wondering what to do. Our bodies ached badly from the prolonged lying on the hard ground.

In retrospect, it became clear to us that on the morning of April 11, SS officers were ordered to evacuate the camp. The members of the political underground understood that the Americans were close and decided that this was the time to revolt. They took control of Buchenwald a few hours before the arrival of the first American tanks at the camp gates. Some underground members approached the fences and began to cut them to allow passage to the SS area of residence. Armed members of the underground took over the camp commander's office and captured dozens of SS. Some German and Ukrainian guards quickly stripped off their uniforms to try to escape to the forests that surrounded the camp and pretend they were civilians. The command of the camp passed in the late morning to the International Committee of the Underground.

In the early afternoon, the German army's flamethrowers unit arrived in Buchenwald. Their mission was to destroy and set fire to the abandoned camp buildings and kill their occupants, if any remained. They were met by members of the underground, weapons in hand, who captured 220 SS men alive.

At 3:15 p.m., the first American tank entered the gates of Buchenwald.

The clock on the camp gate was stopped at this precise time to serve as an eternal testimony.

A call came forth from the camp's public address system – "The camp has been liberated. You are all free."

Shani and I looked at each other in disbelief.

We left our hiding place in the hut and walked out, our eyes squinting hard in the bright light of the day.

Many soldiers walked around the camp, their uniforms different from those we were used to seeing. They surveyed their surroundings and their gaze revealed the intensity of the shock they felt at what they were seeing. A large group of soldiers stood nearby and looked down at a pile of corpses lying near the fence. Their faces expressed shock, and some wept softly in the face of the horrors revealed to their eyes. They looked at us with compassion - an emotion I had not seen or felt for a year.

We walked slowly, happy to be outside and breathe the clean air after the long stay in hiding. Like us, other prisoners began to emerge from their hiding places. In Buchenwald, iron discipline had prevailed and it was strictly forbidden to roam the camp without a purpose. The sight of people moving around freely without gunshots, shouting or beatings illustrated to us more than a thousand words could, that the nightmare was over.

The scene looked like it was out of a film. Bedraggled, gaunt creatures in striped shirts wandered the camp. They walked slowly, aimlessly, their gaze hollow and expressionless. No one smiled.

The freedom we dreamed of had come, but the feeling was very different from what we had imagined.

Our struggle for survival, day by day, hour by hour, had robbed us of the ability to feel.

The same mechanism that had forced us to emotionally disconnect to survive prevented us in that moment we had dreamed of, from feeling true joy. We knew we were free, but it would be many months before our hearts, which had known almost inconceivable sorrow and pain, would truly beat again.

We later learned that when our block was vacated, the camp underground began to take control of the enormous confusion. Most of the children from block 66 had managed to find a hiding place and escape the evacuation. Some climbed into piles of corpses and hid among the dead, while others descended into the camp's underground sewer system. A few were recaptured by the Germans...

We later found out that nearly everyone who was captured and forced to go with the Germans during the evacuation of the camp did not survive.

The terrible hunger we suffered from continued to take its toll even after liberation.

The American soldiers, who arrived in the first tanks in Buchenwald, threw cans of food at the famished prisoners who pounced on every morsel that came to hand. The general onslaught on the food deterred Shani and me from participating. We were exhausted and weak and despite the hunger, we did not feel capable of getting close to the distribution centers and fighting the crowds for the cans of food.

Looking back, this behavior saved our lives. A huge number of survivors who had lived through the atrocities died from health complications in the first days of their release. The food distributed by the American soldiers was canned meat with high levels of fat. After long months and sometimes even years of malnutrition, the freed prisoners' stomachs were unable to digest the fatty meat and they came down with typhus and died a few days later. About 60% of the inmates liberated at Buchenwald died as a result.

Almost every prisoner who rushed for food paid for it with his life.

Shani and I wandered through the abandoned camp. We were hungry, thirsty, and looking for some food in the piles of rubbish around us. We found nothing. We arrived at the building where the SS offices were. Objects were strewn around the area, reflecting the speed at which things were changing. We found some ointment and licked it. It contained a bit of sugar and the sweetness revived us a little. In one of the closets, we found food meant for the camp dogs. It turned out that my first meal, as a free man, was a snack of dog biscuits.

Towards evening, some of the boys called us to come with them to the camp gate.

Among the American soldiers was a rabbi named Herschel Schechter who had come to Buchenwald. He asked to see the children who had survived. Rabbi Schechter was a high-ranking officer, responsible for the welfare of the Jewish soldiers who had fought in the United States army.

We saw great excitement in the rabbi's face. He hurried to hand out to us all prayer books specially issued for the Jewish soldiers in the United States Army. The rabbi also gave us a small pendant in the shape of a mezuzah, and distributed tefillin, prayer shawls, and other accessories and asked us to promise to continue praying.

I lost the pendant over the years, but the prayer book I received in Buchenwald on April 11, 1945, is with me to this day.

Walking around the camp exhausted us. We were very weak, like human shadows. That same evening, the Americans began preparing huge pots of nutritious porridge for us, which gradually restored our bodies to a semblance of health. They advised us to be careful and eat only soups and porridge in a careful, controlled manner.

After dinner, we gathered again at the only place we knew, Block 66.

We lay on the bunks, in a long line. A short time later, a soldier appeared in the doorway of the hut, with a camera in his hand.

The photographer stood there in his American military uniform and surveyed us silently as we lay on the bunks.

From where I lay at the end of the block I saw that some boys were looking into the camera, some were staring at an undefined point and others were looking away intentionally.

Emaciated faces, and almost completely shaven hair. No one smiles.

The sunken eyes looked blank. They were the same eyes that had seen their family members taken away from them forever; eyes that had seen their friends executed for stealing a potato or a vegetable, or had seen them falling in the snow on death marches, or going up in smoke through the camp chimneys.

On the arm of many of the survivors is forever engraved an identity burned into their flesh by the Germans.

The "click" from the camera captured that moment.

The image was a symbol and far more powerful than a thousand words, because even though our bodies were free, our spirits had not yet gone on this journey of sudden freedom. We could not rejoice in our hearts.

During the long years of war, we dreamed of this moment countless times. We tried to remember the taste of freedom; to imagine the moment, to try to survive until it came.

Now, when the day of liberation came, we felt almost lost, perhaps out of habit, or maybe simply because we did not know where to go. We gathered again in the narrow bunks, the only place we could lay our heads at the end of each day, and dreamt of freedom.

We were free but captive to the terrible sights we had witnessed, which would accompany us all our lives.

The photograph that captured the moment in the bunks today hangs on a wall in the Yad Vashem Museum.

The next day they transferred us to a large and comfortable building, which had been used by the SS soldiers. It was a solid structure separated into rooms. Here was where we underwent our initial rehabilitation. The Americans provided us with set meals of nutritious porridge three times a day: morning, noon and evening. Two senior American officers who were sitting not far from us had overheard the conversation between us and understood that we spoke Hungarian. It turned out that one of the officers was originally from Bergsas and Shani knew him well. The American officer was the brother of Dr. Shak, Shani's family doctor. For the first time, we allowed ourselves to feel a longing for home.

I was ill during the first days after my release. The infection on my legs was bothering me again and my body temperature was rising. My legs were swollen and I had difficulty standing on my feet.

Shani went to look for a quiet corner for me where I could lie down. Not far away was a sports hall and a tennis court that had been used by the SS. In the corner of the hall was a small cubicle with two beds without a mattress. There was a nearby wood stove. Shani supported me and helped me get to the room and lie down. He then went outside, found pieces of wood and cigarettes, and lit a fire that heated the room.

The next day, many prisoners went on a tour of the camp organized by the American soldiers. I was not physically fit for this. In retrospect, it dawned on me that my incapacity to participate had spared me from having to see very difficult sights, which my comrades saw. In many areas, there were piles of discarded corpses which the Nazis did not manage to burn.

Shani continued wandering alone to remote areas of the camp, where we were denied access. He was always more curious than I, and had a strong wish to see everything with his own eyes. Hidden from view, my friend found the crematorium where the Nazis incinerated hundreds of bodies every day of prisoners who had died in the camp.

These horrific images are with him even today, 75 years after the end of the war.

An American doctor treated me with pills and in a few days, I regained my strength. In one of the offices in the camp, I found a notebook, and began to document some of my experiences. Unfortunately, I later lost it.

The U.S. military was careful to document and transmit to the world all the atrocities they discovered in the camp.

On April 15, four days after Buchenwald's liberation, radio journalist Edward R. Murrow aired a special broadcast from the camp to his listeners in the following words:

"I pray for you to believe what I have said about Buchenwald. I reported what I saw and heard, but only part of it. For most of it, I have no words. If I have offended you by this rather mild account of Buchenwald, I'm not in the least bit sorry..."

The descriptions and sights that flowed to the West were the first and most horrific visual evidence of what had happened in Europe under Nazi German rule. General George S. Patton, who headed the 6th Army and whose troops liberated Buchenwald, gathered some 2,000 inhabitants from the nearby town of Weimar, and marched them the few miles that separated their comfortable lives from Buchenwald's hell. He made them see for themselves the atrocities perpetrated by their government. The residents of Weimar, well dressed and smiling as they entered the camp, are seen in a film produced by the American army, stunned and expressing deep shock.

On the day of the liberation of the camp, I was 14 and a half and weighed about 35 kilograms.

I felt like I had been born twice:

The first time on September 21, 1930.

The second time on April 11, 1945.

Along with me, another 903 children were reborn: my friends in Block 66.

Every year we all celebrate our common birthday.

No balloons. No cake. No pleasure… |And without many of our family members, who did not get to be there on the day of liberation.

50 years after the liberation of the Buchenwald camp, on April 11, 1995, we gathered at the press house in Tel Aviv; the camp's survivors, including the children of Block 66.

Rabbi Israel Lau was an 8-year-old boy who was staying in a block of non-Jewish prisoners, where his older brother, Naftali, had managed to sneak him. He was released along with us. In his speech at the conference, he said that all of us there, who were born on different dates and in different places - were celebrating a second birthday together: 50 years old.

It is without question that we owed our lives to Antonin Kalina, a Czech communist and a veteran of Buchenwald, and perhaps this is the place to give him the respect and gratitude he so deserves.

Antonin Kalina was born in 1902 to an impoverished family of ten children in the Czech city of Częstochowa, which had a large Jewish community. From a young age, he had to go out to work to help support his family, and he developed into a sturdy and robust young man. He had no formal education but he was an intelligent man and through self-study he mastered several languages, including German.

Kalina adopted Communist principles and participated in struggles and demonstrations for the workers of his city. When the Nazis took over Czechoslovakia, they arrested him and sent him to Dachau. In 1939, he was transferred to Buchenwald, where he managed to survive thanks to the excellent German he had acquired on his own. There, he became active in the camp underground.

At the beginning of 1945, many hundreds of hungry and weak Jewish boys who had survived the death marches arrived in Buchenwald. The political prisoners described the children who came to the camp as "half dead." Kalina and his friends were shocked by their appearance and decided to do everything they could to save the children. They saw in them the future after the war. Among those enlisted to help the children was Jack Weber, a Jewish political prisoner who had been in Buchenwald since 1939 and was a member of the underground. Jack's wife and baby daughter were murdered and he had lost interest in life until the group of young Jewish boys arrived. Their rescue operation was a balm for his grieving soul.

Kalina came up with the idea of housing the children in a separate block, at the refuse-filled edge of the camp, located in the heart of a swamp and away from the watchful eye of the Germans. Kalina made sure the children were not forced to work by spreading a rumor that typhus was raging in their barracks. He obtained another significant benefit for the children by transferring the morning and evening roll-calls to the inside of the building and in an abbreviated manner that included only counting instead of standing for long hours with the camp inmates, in the freezing outdoors.

Kalina did all he could to improve the harsh living conditions. Although he was a prisoner himself, he demanded from the German who was in charge of supplies to get 2000 blankets. Thus, he managed to create a situation where each boy got two blankets. Most of the children remained silent in light of these significant gestures. Kalina understood. He said that the children had gone through such terrible trauma: some of them seeing their parents or siblings slaughtered before their eyes. Their silence was understandable.

When the Germans began to prepare for the evacuation of the camp, Kalina gathered all the children in the block and changed their shirts, which had the Jewish identification badge. He asked them to remember that they were Christian Poles, and under no circumstances would they respond to the German call, when it came. Kalina even threatened the children that he would beat any child who said he is Jewish.

When SS soldiers broke into the children's barracks the next morning and ordered Kalina to send all the Jews to the parade ground, he stood before them fearlessly and said emphatically that there were no more Jews in the block. He showed the Nazi commander paperwork prepared ahead of time with the help of friends, which showed the children were registered Christians. 22,000 Jewish prisoners had been sent from Buchenwald on death marches since April 6. Kalina was able to rescue 904 children from the clutches of the Germans thanks to his courage, resourcefulness and determination.

Among the boys saved by Kalina were two who would later become Nobel laureates: Eli Wiesel and the Hungarian writer Imra Curtis.

After the end of the war, Kalina returned to his home country and continued his life in anonymity.

The boys he had saved, like many Holocaust survivors, threw themselves into trying to rebuild their lives and put behind them the years of horror. The trauma they experienced and the loss of near and distant relatives, and their entire childhood world accompanied them like a shadow. In an effort to focus on life, many of them remained silent for many years.

In the sole interview he gave to a pair of American journalists in 1988, Kalina shrugged when asked about the huge rescue operation for which he was responsible. He did not see it as a great achievement, beyond his duty as a human being. He said, "I had already lived my life; their lives were still ahead of them."

This interview is the only photographic testimony left of a great and humble man.

Kalina died of cancer in 1990, at the age of 88, in obscurity.

He never told anyone of his close associates and the amazing rescue story he was in charge of, and expected nothing for it.

The first time his story became public was in 2009. Stanislav Motel, a journalist with an investigative program on Czech television, aired the story. In 2013, he published a book called "Kalina's Children,", which was made into a documentary.

Stephen Moskowitz, the son of one of the boys Kalina saved, created another film entitled "The Children of Block 66."

In 2012, after pressure from several survivors andled by Naftali (Duro) Furst, one of the children of Block 66, Kalina was recognized as a Righteous Among the Nations by Yad Vashem. In 2014, twenty-four years after his death, an impressive ceremony was held in Prague Castle where Kalina was posthumously awarded a medal of honor by the President of the Czech Republic.

In 2017, his story was made public in the Israeli newspaper Yedioth Ahronoth with the headline "The Angel of the Buchenwald Children."

Many years after his death, Kalina gained the recognition and respect he deserved, and was nicknamed the "Czech Schindler."

Businessman Oscar Schindler saved about 1,200 Jews as a free and well-to-do man, with close links to the authorities. Antonin Kalina was himself a prisoner, facing real and immediate danger to his life, and yet he proactively and independently led one of the largest rescue operations during the Holocaust.

Many generations of the descendants of the 903 boys he saved owe their lives to the Christian Kalina, this brave and worthy Czech.

Where many found it difficult to maintain their humanity, Kalina was a human being in the fullest meaning of the word.

Left: Antonin Kalina in his younger years.
Right: Antonin Kalina, from a press article in 2017

The inscription on the gate of the Buchenwald camp –
"Every man to his fate." Ironically, it was in this camp that
the rescue operation initiated by the camp underground
took place, thanks to which over 900 Jewish children
survived.

The Journey Home

We remained in Buchenwald for about four weeks, until our bodies began getting stronger.

After this period, the American doctors thought that we were strong enough to leave the camp. The Buchenwald children received an offer to immigrate to the United States and build a new life overseas, away from the continent of Europe, which was full of traumatic memories. Most of the youngsters had lost their families during the war, and had no home to go back to. Quite a few of the children decided to choose this option.

As for me, there was only one decision. I wanted to go home, to Bergsas.

I knew that I might not find any of my family there, but I felt a strong urge to return to where I grew up and find out what happened to them.

The first stop they took us to when we left Buchenwald was a convalescent home in Prague, where we were furnished identity papers. We also ate fuller meals, which no longer endangered us after our stomachs had adapted to raw food.

One day a soldier in a Czech army uniform arrived at the convalescent home. I was told he was looking for me.

I approached until I stood in front of him and we recognized each other.

It was my cousin, Moshe Lazarowitz.

Moshe Lazarowitz in Czech Army Uniform

Moshe worked with my father in the factory and in 1942, when my father was drafted into the labor battalions, Moshe remained in Bergsas to help run the factory. Moshe's father was not drafted because he was too old at the time.

Later, in 1943, Moshe also had to enlist.

Moshe managed to avoid the Hungarian labor battalions and joined the Czech underground army, where he fought against the Germans with the partisans in the forests. At a certain point, the Czechs set up an army consisting of labor battalions of Czech origin. After the surrender of Germany and the liberation of Europe, these fighters became soldiers in the regular Czech army.

When lists of survivors of the concentration and extermination camps in the Prague area were published, Moshe found my name among them and hurried to look for me. It had been more than two years since he left for the labor battalions, and I had never seen him in uniform. He, too, had difficulty recognizing the boy he knew in the scrawny boy he now saw before him.

It was an emotional encounter. We soon compared stories of what had happened to us since we last met.

Moshe asked only general questions: whom I saw, about whom I had heard... I chose not to go into the stories in depth and was content with a general description of what I had gone through.

Moshe asked permission to take me out of the convalescent home for a few hours. He was the supply officer of his unit and had the use of a military vehicle. About half an hour's drive from the convalescent home was the camp where Moshe served and by virtue of his rank, he had complete access to the unit's well-stocked storeroom.

As we entered the base kitchen, my eyes widened at the abundance.

Moshe looked at me kindly.

"Tell me what you are allowed and what you are not allowed to eat and I will make sure they prepare anything you want."

I tried to think. Almost automatically, I said "pasta with poppy seeds."

It was a dish from my parents' house, and as a child, I loved the combination of poppy seeds, sugar, and pasta cooked in sauce. Moshe called the cook, who prepared a platter of pasta for me, exactly per my request.

Over the years, every time I recalled this meal, which brought back to my stomach and my heart the flavors of home, my eyes filled with tears.

After the meal, Moshe took me back to the convalescent home.

A few more weeks passed, and we felt healthy enough to get going.

We were a bunch of kids, lost in the world.

As I mentioned, many boys preferred to accept the Americans' offer and traveled to the United States. Their desire to move away from Europe was strong, and the past was saturated with loss and suffering. Some sought to wipe away their Jewish identity, trying to shed the years of terror and trauma that accompanied them at the end of the war and many years beyond.

One of these boys was Alberger, whom we knew from Burgsas and met on the train car to Buchenwald. It was his father who made sure to talk to us and warned us not to fall asleep on the way. After the war, Alberger and his father decided to immigrate to the United States. For a while, we kept in touch by letter, until one day I received a letter from him with a request to cease all contact between us. As part of his determined decision to stay away from Judaism, Alberger had married a Christian girl and tried to wipe out all connection to the past. His relationship with me was too painful a reminder for him...

As I mentioned, when we had to decide where we were going, I had no hesitation. I was going to return to my hometown. I could not imagine going anywhere else without finding out what happened to my family.

Shani felt the same, and there were a few other boys from Bergsas who decided to join us. We received the required documents for the trip, and enough money to reach our destination.

Returning 'home' was not easy.

We had to find a train heading in the direction of Bergsas. It was the beginning of July, about two months after the end of the war. Europe was still bleeding and most of the transportation infrastructure was damaged in the areas where fighting took place.

Refugees seeking to return home packed the train stations and there was virtually no room on the trains. There were very few trains, and those that did operate filled up to capacity.

We somehow managed to board one of them, terribly crowded. We were eight boys on our way home.

I did not know what would await me at home. Who would be there if anyone...

The uncertainty that had been with me all through the war was now stirring my most sensitive inner self.

I took care to suppress my thoughts in order to endure the emotions that flooded over me.

I did not know what I would find in my house. Did any of my family members survive?

More frightening was the fear of knowing which of them I would never see again.

In the emotional loneliness that accompanied the long separation from my parents and brother there was only one person with me: Shani. Our long journey together was about to end when we got home. From the moment of our release, no one who could separate us; Shani and I were like brothers. In the chaos all around, we held to each other like an anchor.

We knew that even if our paths should part, we would forever be connected in a strong bond.

In that world that we have tried over the years to leave behind, he was the only person who had really been there with me, and understands what I went through.

To this day, I consider him a brother.

Today we are both close to ninety, but in some ways, we are still and always will be 13-14 years old. When we managed to squeeze onto the crowded train, I saw people sitting on the roof of the car as well. I suggested to my friends that we join them so we would be outside and suffer less from the crowding and lack of air inside. We had little chance of finding a place in the car anyway. We climbed onto the roof of the train and found a corner to sit with some comfort, despite the overcrowding. The train locomotive emitted sparks from the burning coal while traveling. These flew over us and burned small holes in my shirt.

Before the war, I would not have imagined climbing on top of a train for such a long trip. The resourcefulness that had guided me in making various decisions during the war had once again come to my aid.

In a circuitous, complicated journey, we traveled towards home. We had to board several different trains, and the trip was a long one.

When we finally neared Bergsas' central station, we were told to get ready to get off in a few minutes.

I was home…

The train gradually slowed down and finally stopped at the station. I did not recognize the place I knew so well.

I got off slowly. A year and three months had passed since we left the house, not knowing where we were heading…

We left one world, and I had returned to another.

I was standing on the platform, at our train station: the familiar place I came to every summer to go to my grandparents' house in the village.

I did not take notice that I had stopped and stood still, rooted to the spot. Behind me, other people continued pouring off the train.

Images flashed before my eyes…The ones I had pushed out of my mind for so long.

Mom, my little brother, and I quickly leave the house, Mom's hands holding ours tightly. She has a bag on her shoulder with some food inside she had managed to pack for us. We had passed through this very street, on our way to the ghetto.

When we left home, I had a family. I was a child.

That childhood ended a few weeks later, on another train platform, when I had to let go of my mother's hand.

The images kept running before my eyes… The past, the present, reality and imaginings - all jumbled together.

For months, I dreamed of the moment when I would return home.

But I never thought that when that moment came -

I would feel I was suffocating,

Sad…

And completely alone in the world.

Commotion was all around me, trains blaring as they entered the station, people running everywhere trying to find lost relatives, shouting out their names in hopes that someone would answer, to give them some information about what had become of their loved ones.

And I? I stood there, planted in place, staring at the rubble around me, at the effects of the bombings on the walls of the bombed-out station, at the forlorn shops on the street - some of which were still empty, desolate.

This place does not look like my home, the one I left, and to which I was longing to return.

There were many people waiting on the platform, greeting those of us getting off the trains, hoping to get a glimmer of information about their lost loved ones.

They asked where we were from, and called out to us "Have you seen…?" "Did you ever come across...?" "Do you know what happened to...?"

We started moving towards the city, making our way through the swarms of people, trying to get to the town center -near the Great Synagogue. From a distance, we saw a crowd of many Jews there.

Now it was our turn to ask questions - each one about his family.

Someone told me that my cousin Ilona was in Bergsas, staying in the apartment of her relatives, the Berkowitz family. I knew that home; it was right in front of the Great Synagogue. I started to go in that direction but even before I could reach it - I found my cousin in the crowd. Like the others, she too had heard that a train full of refugees was arriving and she went out to check if any of our family members would be on it.

We hugged each other. It was very moving for both of us.

Ilo told me that when she returned to Bergsas from Buda-pest she found that her uncle's apartment in the city center was empty; they had not returned. Many Jews who came back were looking for places to stay, and she moved into the abandoned apartment and waited, hoping that more family members would return. The apartment's proximity to the city center and the train station enabled her to check whenever a train arrived, to see if any family members were on it.

We walked together to the apartment. I looked around. Returning to the streets of my childhood was difficult. I had left a vibrant city, full of energy and life. In the city center, which was always crowded, there were many deserted shops, and the general atmosphere was oppressive and gloomy. In pain, I realized that the world I had known before the war was gone forever. The old life I had been waiting to return to was now only a memory.

"Moishe" Ilo looked at me excitedly, with teary eyes, "Your mother is alive."

My heart stopped, I looked up at her.

"She went to Bucharest and will be back in a few days." She told me.

Ilona explained that in Bucharest, they were distributing some goods to survivors and mother went to receive them.

I would like to say that I was happy and excited to hear this news, but I am not sure that happened.

I mostly sensed that I could not feel anything.

It had been fifteen months since I had left Mom when she assured me that it was all right to move to the second column.

Fifteen months, since the figures of Mother and Arnold had moved away from me and I was alone.

In those long, dreadful months, I had trained myself not to feel anything, and to concentrate only on survival.

Now came this moment, where I was supposed to be emotionally overwhelmed, filled with happiness, bursting with joy…And I felt nothing.

I did not ask what had happened to my little brother.

I knew.

The next morning when I got up, I went to see our house on Seicheni Street.

I made my way across the street, with hesitant caution. I stood and gazed at the familiar structure.

Our house after the war

The house where I had spent my happy childhood was no longer the same. The Russian army had set up a large kitchen for the soldiers to use in the compound. Huge stoves were scattered throughout our residential building for military use.

We could not return. That was clear. Nothing there reminded me of the house we had left behind when they sent us to the ghetto.

I heard a mocking voice behind me, "Look, little Kessler is back."

It was the Hungarian woman neighbor in the house next to ours, the Kudebitz family.

She glared at me scornfully and pointed her finger. A shiver went through my body.

The insult washed over me. I walked away in silence, her cynical laughter echoing.

It was where I had grown up, but it was no longer a home for me.

I waited for Mom four or five days until she arrived one morning.

Seeing her again was the hardest thing for me.

Even today, when I think about it, tears well up in my eyes.

We had not seen each other for more than a year since that quick parting on the platform at Auschwitz before Satan's penetrating eyes. A whole year in which we had each lived on a separate planet. She had no idea that her eldest son had survived the war.

When Mom arrived, I was still asleep. Ilona told her I had returned....

She rushed to where I was, stood in the doorway, unbelieving, and saw me asleep.

She woke me up, and hugged me tightly to her bosom. Her body was trembling and tears poured from her eyes uncontrollably.

Seventy-five years have gone by since that moment. Even today, it is etched in my soul and the memory inundates my heart. The image is clear before my eyes, and the years fall away.

Mom weeps, hugs me tight, looks at me, and cannot believe it.

And I? I felt nothing.

I know Mom was waiting to feel like I was hers, to know that she had a family again.

But I could not, I just could not give that to her.

"Why are you crying, Mom?" I asked gently. Mother looked at me through her tears and was silent. She could not stop the tears.

"I can no longer cry." I whispered, half to myself, half to her.

I could not give back to my mother the love she so desperately wanted from me.

My emotions had died there, on the platform at Birkenau, at the moment I was left alone, solely responsible for my fate.

Mom told me in a quivering voice what had happened to her since we parted.

I looked into her eyes and saw the profound sadness there as she told me that my little brother was no more.

A few minutes after we had parted at the train platform, the Germans split the queue she stood in with Arnold into three: young, healthy women, older women, and children. The Germans wanted to use all the labor they could for the war effort and did not hesitate to separate mothers from their tender young children.

Mom and Rosie, my father's sister, were sent to one side, while Grandma, my little brother, and my three little cousins - Rosie's children - were sent to another column. My little brother was taken from my mother even before they reached the end of the selection in Birkenau. It all happened very fast, with urgency, shouting, and clamor.

That was the last time she saw Arnold. She had no idea at that moment that he was doomed. Only a few days later it became clear to her that all the children had been exterminated immediately and that her little son was dead.

My younger brother was eight years old at the time of his death.

Only a few hours after our train arrived at its destination he was no longer alive. I do not know if in his last moments anyone from our family was with him. I hope our grandmother, and our cousins were…

The column to which they sent Mother after being separated from my brother was intended for work.

Mother passed the selection, and like me, waited in Auschwitz for several days until she received a number and was sent to the women's concentration camp, Ravensbruck.

Mother went through her horrific journey together with my aunt Rosie, who was married to Isidore Kessler, Dad's brother. They had three small children aged 6-10 and there was a close family bond between the two families. We would meet every Saturday and on every holiday, as we attended the same synagogue.

In 1942, they drafted Isidore into the labor battalions and Rosie remained at home with the children. They moved to the ghetto and were loaded with us on the train to Auschwitz. In that terrible selection, on the platform in Birkenau, they also separated Rosie from her three children.

Hani, dad's sister who was with them on the platform, was sent for extermination with my cousins, Magda and Zulik.

Rosie and Mom, left alone, clung to each other and remained close from that moment on.

After the interim period in Auschwitz, my mother and aunt were sent to a concentration camp in Germany for women only: Ravensbruck. The women in the camp worked hard in an ammunition factory nearby and served German industry. Living conditions were extremely difficult and over time gas chambers were built and it became an extermination camp.

Towards the end of the war, Ravensbruck was evacuated and the inmates, including Mother and Rosie, were sent on death marches. Those who survived were freed by the United States military when they arrived at the Gunskirchen camp.

Like me, Mother had struggled for many months with severe and constant hunger, abuse by SS guards, extremely hard physical work, and deep uncertainty about the fate of her family. I am sure that her days were also accompanied by deep pain, which resulted from the clear knowledge that her little boy had been sent to his death without her being able to protect him and save him from the cruel fate that awaited him.

In the next few days, we spent hours together and I gradually learned about what had happened to the whole family.

Mother told me that a few hours after we arrived in Birkenau, Rosie and Isidore's three children were murdered along with my grandmother and little brother. Rosie never got over the cruel and immediate loss of her three children. After Mom and Rosie managed to get to Bergsas, Rosie learned that her husband, Isidore, was alive. Of the family they had started together, only the parent couple remained.

Rosie and Isidore decided to move away from Europe and emigrate as far as possible, to the United States. There they hoped to restore their wounded souls. They did their best to start over and rebuild their lives, in the shadow of the terrible loss of their three young children. The tragedy has accompanied them all their lives.

They later had one child, Harold. Isidore and Rosie kept silent over the years and their son knew nothing about their experiences in the war, other than the fact that his mother had been in in Auschwitz. Evidence of this was tattooed on her arm. Isidore turned to Real Estate and became financially well off. He used to say that if a person was selling needles, he would end up with some needles, while if a person was selling Real Estate, he would end up with a few houses.

Isidore was a Zionist activist and came to Israel on several visits as part of his activities. Rosie joined him after much persuasion for just one or two visits. Despite her attempt to erase the trauma and give her son a good life, far from the horrors she went through and the immense loss she experienced - a large part of Rosie remained in the past, and was unable to fully recover and return to life.

Influenced by his mother, Harold grew up disconnected from Judaism and Israel. He also did not want to have a Bar Mitzvah celebration, which his father wanted to hold in Israel.

It was only after Harold grew up and his parents died that he decided to visit Israel himself. He wanted to investigate his roots and find out more about the family history from which he had been cut off. When we met, he told me how much he had suffered from his mother's depressions, which he did not fully comprehend.

After Rosie's death, Harold was shocked to discover that he had three brothers who were separated from his mother and had perished in Auschwitz. This information must have helped him better understand his mother's anguished soul, even after her death.

Family was very important to their son Harold, and on each visit to Israel, he would ask me to invite the whole family for a meal, so that he could know the next generation of the Kessler family in Israel.

Harold now lives in Miami, continuing his father's business. He is married and has two children. Harold's daughter, Clara, is named after both of our grandmothers and we maintain a close bond.

Let us return to Bergsas, in the summer of 1945.

Mom and I spent most of the day together, talking and filling in the gaps.

Mom spoke mostly about the forced labor in the factory. I'm certain she tried to spare me her worst experiences…And I did the same; so as not to upset her I told her about what I had gone through only in general terms. Most of the Jews who came back from the camps tried as much as possible to avoid delving deeply into the bitter memories and traumas they had suffered. The main thing was that they had survived; no one asked questions of how or why…

One day we decided to go back to our house together, to look for the valuables we had buried in the wood warehouse before we were expelled from the house. We dug in a place where we had hid, among other things, candlesticks and other silverware. In the warehouse soil we saw clear signs of excavation and nothing was there in the hiding place. People from our neighborhood had probably taken advantage of the house standing empty, and looted our valuables. Some neighbors safe-guarded the possessions of the Jewish families they had quickly hidden before leaving in April 1944. Others rushed in to loot the empty houses.

Mom and I realized that there was no point in returning to this place, which only a year and a half ago was our home. We went back to the apartment and tried to think what the best thing was for us to do next.

One question still remained unanswered for me: what had happened to Dad?

I did not ask Mom anything about him and she did not volunteer any information. Refugees were still coming home from all over Europe and I hoped my father would be among them.

A few weeks later my mother told me.

As soon as she returned home, Mother wrote to her sisters in Dobřenice, hoping that one of them had come back. She was overjoyed to learn that three of her sisters - Rosie, Helen and Iren - had survived.

The story unraveled slowly…

Mother's two unmarried sisters, Helen and Iren, and Mother's younger brother, Jacob, were deported from Dobřenice to Auschwitz with their father. Rosie, the married sister - was also expelled from her home and the three sisters met in Bergen-Belsen.

My grandfather and Jacob -my mother's brother - did not survive.

Rosie, Helen and Iren went through the war together, in the Bergen-Belsen camp. When the camp was evacuated, they were taken on death marches to another camp, where they were freed and stayed to recover.

Two days before the end of the war, they met my father.

By coincidence my father passed through the area in retreat from the front with the Hungarian labor battalions in which he was still enlisted. At an overnight site near the camp, Dad was stunned to meet Mom's three sisters his sisters-in-law. They were all thrilled. Dad was in charge of the army kitchen and promised to come to the camp the next day with a supply of food for them.

He never made it.

Mom's sisters found out that the next day, Dad was walking down the street in the same area where they met. A few hours before the official end of the war, random shots were fired in the street and one of them hit him in the chest. Dad was taken to an American military hospital in the nearest town.

He was hospitalized but was unable to recover from the critical injury and died. One of the hospital employees collected his identity papers, and when Mother's sisters tried to find out why he hadn't shown up, his comrades in the labor battalion told them he had been shot. This is how it became clear to them, and later to my mother, what had happened to Dad.

The photograph found in my father, Herman's pocket, in
May 1945 when he lay dying in the hospital. Someone who
recognized him, took his documents and asked that they
be sent to the family. And that way, we understood what
had happened to him.

My father survived three years of grueling hard labor, risking
his life every day.

A single stray bullet took his life on the last day of the war.

Mother's three sisters managed to return to Užhorod, the
capital of the Carpathian region. There, they parted ways:
Rosie, who was married, returned to her home in the city and

reunited with her husband. Helen and Iren returned to their house in Dobřenice.

It was clear to all of them that Jacob, their younger brother, had not survived. He was a few years older than Iren.

Mother's older sisters, Miriam and Sarna, who were deported in 1942 when their husbands' families could not prove Hungarian citizenship, had perished in the killing pits of Kaminski Podolsk.

When the sisters heard that my mother had come back home, they contacted her and told her what had happened to Dad. Mother decided not to tell me right away in order to give me time to recover physically and emotionally. She realized that the loss of my little brother and the trauma I had experienced would hit me hard, and she wanted to spare me the knowledge that my father was never coming back.

After living in Dobřenice for a while and realizing that no more family members would be returning, Helen and Iren came to Bergsas and stayed with us for a while in the spacious apartment. When they arrived, Mom decided it was time to tell me about Dad; she could not continue to protect me from the painful truth.

For the first time, I wept.

The war had taken my grandmother, my grandfather, my little cousins, uncles and aunts…

…my little brother

…and my father

And it had taken my belief in man and in God.

It had stripped me of my childhood innocence.

I had been troubled that it also had taken my ability to feel.

With the tears I shed for my dead father, I came back to life.

Years later, I took a trip to Austria and decided to do more in-depth research about my father's war experiences and the exact location of his death. I wanted to pay my last respects to him and bring his bones to Israel.

I knew that my father had been treated at an American hospital near the Austrian city of Linz. I was hoping that there would be a grave marking in place. For several months I gathered every bit of information about the hospital where my father was taken. There was no internet at the time and it was very difficult to uncover archives with lists of names of those hospitalized there.

On my next visit to Austria I traveled to where the American Hospital was located, in the city of Wels. I was able to locate lists of Hungarian labor battalion soldiers who had been treated and died. The hospital staff was sympathetic and tried to help me, but unfortunately, I did not find Dad's name on the lists. I went through the details of the 1,032 deceased, among them about 120 were listed as "unidentified." I knew for certain that my father had been treated at this hospital because the evidence was unequivocal. After being shot in the chest, my father was evacuated by the Americans who occupied the city where he was shot, and took him to the nearest hospital located near the Austrian city of Linz. It was still a wartime atmosphere and many of those who died in the hospital did not receive personal burial, but were buried in a mass grave in a nearby Christian cemetery. In the first days after the war, many people died, and the authorities did not engage in individual burials at all.

I was told that a monument had been erected on the site, commemorating the victims of the war. After an extensive search I located the monument, which was completely covered with climbing vegetation. It was obvious that no one had visited the place for years. I assume that many families do not even know that their lost relatives may be in this mass grave. I cleared off the monument and saw a sign that read: "In Memory of 1,032 War Victims." The grass around me was growing over a mass grave. I would not be able to bring Dad's bones to Israel.

It was a difficult moment for me, knowing that my father had been buried without any sign of his individual character and uniqueness. One of the goals of the Germans in the war was to erase the personal identity of the Jews and turn them into numbers. Although they had lost the war, my father's character and very being, as well as those of countless others, were obliterated with his death. His name is not even written on a tombstone. He left this world anonymously, one number among 1032 others, faceless and without identity.

I decided to set up a tombstone on the grass with a memorial plaque. There were already a few there that had been placed by individual families in memory of their loved ones. I turned to one of the workers at the place and paid him a considerable sum of money to prepare such a tombstone for me. It is there to this day.

The memorial plaque I commissioned in memory of my father on the mass grave in Austria.

I have never had a grave to visit on a regular basis and give my father the respect he deserves, but knowing that his name exists at the site where he was buried gave me some comfort. Recently, Linz's Jewish community erected a monument there, and I placed a memorial candle on it.

My father had three sisters and a brother before the war broke out.

Of the five, only his brother Isidore survived. We were both the last remnants of the Kessler family.

Life after the war

For the first few months after the war, I lived with my mother at Ilona's uncle's house in the city center. Many survivors returned to the city, searching for family members. In most cases the search was in vain. From large, extensive families, only a few survivors remained.

As I have mentioned, Iren, my mother's younger sister, came to live with us for a while in the period following the war. In Bergsas she met her future husband, Zvi Saks.

Zvi's older brother, Moshe, was already in Czechoslovakia and ran one of the German owned farms, which had been abandoned. In May 1945, immediately after the surrender of Nazi Germany, Czechoslovakia took over the rural Sudetenland, which had been annexed by Nazi Germany, and sent the ethnic German population by train to Germany. Following the expulsion of the residents, the Czechoslovakian government confiscated their many assets and declared them government property. The survivors who returned from the camps were given an opportunity by the government to settle on these former German farms, in exchange for their management.

We spoke a great deal about the possibility of immigrating to Israel; we all felt we needed to leave this blood-saturated soil and the painful memories, and build ourselves a new life. In the meantime, Moshe Sacks suggested we move to the farm and work the land.

After a while, we learned that the borders were closing and it would not be possible to move freely between countries. We did not yet know that we were living in an area that would be included in the communist bloc and that the Iron Curtain was about to descend on Eastern Europe and restrict all entry and exit for almost fifty years.

It was clear to us that we did not want to remain under communist rule. We realized we had to hurry and implement our plan before the Soviet Union closed its borders.

Zvi Saks, Iren's intended husband, said he had an acquaintance that could help them cross the border safely and escape. Isaac, another Sacks brother, was going to join us.

Mom convinced me that I should go with Saks and cross the border with him. She promised to follow me.

Once again, we parted ways.

I went to the Sudetenland with Isaac Saks. There were still no secured, sealed border fences and we were able to cross the border late at night relatively easily. We settled on a spacious German farm. Iren and Isaac would live on another large farm in the area.

Mother arrived two or three months later with her new partner, Zev (Wilhelm) Weinberger.

She asked me to sit with her for a talk. She told me that throughout the war she was sure that my father was dead and had said goodbye to him in her heart long before she learned that he had been killed on the final day of the war. When Mother met Wilhelm, who had lost his wife and children in the war and was alone, she saw this as an opportunity to rebuild her life.

Mother knew that her marriage to Zev would finally and painfully end the family we had before the war and that it might hurt me. She asked for my approval, to make sure I did not object.

I was 15 and seemingly an adult, but in the depths of my heart there was a burning pain at the loss of my childhood, and especially at the breakup of my family.

I understood my mother. I saw many people around me who had lost their spouses in the war and were looking to start a new family, which would help them rebuild their lives and move on. The loneliness and loss were hard on everyone.

I replied to Mother that she should do what she understood was right for her. I had a hard time giving her my full support and feeling happy for her, but I did not want to deprive Mom of happiness and the serenity she sought for her soul.

Soon after, Mom and Zev got married on the farm.

I lived with Mom and Zev on another farm that was consigned to us. Iren and her husband, Zvi Saks, ran the farm with us. I helped with various jobs until we made a decision that we needed to get ready for immigration to Israel, and I would need to learn a profession to support me in our new home.

I moved to the city of Goblonz. At the age of 15, I rented an apartment by myself in the city center, about 50-60 kilometers from the farm where we lived. I was still a teenager, but older than my years. I started studying at the jewelry design school, which also included hands on training. I liked the studies and the profession; they were for me an anchor back to a normal life, as much as possible. The factory manager, Misha Bressler, was a Jew, but there were no other Jews in the class I attended. There were only a few Jews in the city, as was the case in many places after the war. After three years I graduated, passed a professional exam, and earned my certificate.

There was great famine in the post-war world, and there was a shortage of food in many places. Luckily, on the farm, Mom and Zev raised chickens that laid eggs and in addition, there were cows, horses and carts. They grew a variety of crops in the fields. Every week I went to the farm and stocked up on food which was expensive in the city. Mom ran the farm kitchen and helped with various tasks. After about two years, Mom and Zev moved and managed a larger farm, which was closer to the town where I studied and lived.

Prior to our immigration to Israel, we traveled to take part in a training program.

It was in 1948, the period of Israel's War of Independence. The training program was held the in the mountains, where we learned how to fight with knives and other means of self-defense. At the end of 1948 we set off, and after waiting in Genoa, Italy, we boarded a ship called TETA that was literally a wreck. The voyage was quite long, and I remember it mostly as being crowded and boring.

We arrived at the port of Haifa in January 1949: Mother, my stepfather, and me.

There was still an atmosphere of war in the country. From the trip, I remember loading our luggage on the roof of the old Egged bus we were traveling in, and the many roadblocks set up on the roads. Most of the young men were drafted into the army as soon as they got off the ship and were sent directly to the front, sometimes without any training. I was given a one-year deferral because I was an only child.

The bus from the port of Haifa brought us to an immigrant camp in Beer Yaakov, with tents. Mother's older brother, Haim Blauvstein, who immigrated to Israel in 1938 and lived in Ramat Gan, came to visit us the next day. When he saw our living conditions, he invited us to stay at his house. We were happy for the offer and moved to his apartment in Ramat Gan, where we remained until we were eligible for our own one-room apartment.

It was very crowded in my uncle's apartment. When the container we had sent from abroad with our possessions arrived, we had it placed in an open field near my uncle's home, and I moved into the container. I lived in a space without windows, and for air to get in on the steamy summer days I left the door slightly open. Jackals came at night and tried to enter, until I chased them off. They scared me and bothered me but I was happy to live in a place of my own in peace and privacy.

In those days in Israel, my field of work was not developed and so I abandoned the idea of working in jewelry in favor of physical work assembling screws. In December 1950 my recruitment deferment ended.

Enlistment into the army was the most important stage in my mental rehabilitation since the end of the war.

After the dreadful helplessness I went through in the camps during the war years, now I took up arms.

I knew that if someone tried to harm me, this time I could defend myself and fight back.

It is hard to describe the intensity of the emotion that welled up in me when I donned the uniform of the Israel Defense Forces, holding my weapon.

Proud, in my IDF uniform

The proud soldier I became was a balm for the soul of the boy prisoner I had been.

My military assignment was in weaponry. I took a professional course and became responsible for the operation of light and heavy arms. My compulsory service was two and a half years, and I was happy to contribute to a country that has become a real home for me.

The State of Israel has been a restorative haven for many survivors. A sense of belonging, self-worth, collective defense, and security gradually healed our wounded souls. Many times during this period, when I was holding a weapon, the question crossed my mind: what would have happened if we had had weapons in those days, when we were helpless in the face of abuse, humiliation and slaughter. How different would our lives have been if we'd had the opportunity to defend ourselves.

The prisoner uniform of the camps had robbed me of my independence and dishonored my religion. It was a humiliating assault on my mind and body in every way.

The IDF uniform gave me pride in my Judaism, my people and in my new homeland.

Moreover, the army gave me a real feeling of belonging: to Israel, Zionism, and patriotism. All of this was added to by a sense of pride in my native homeland, Czechoslovakia. Czech arms made a crucial contribution to Israel's victory in the War of Independence.

Before my enlistment, I joined a youth group from Kadima, which grew out of the rise of Zionist youth. The group consisted of vibrant young men and women who initiated and organized social activities and trips around the country.

On Hanukkah, I was on leave from basic training and glad to discover that the members of the group had organized a dance in the halls of the General Zionist Building in Tel Aviv. The orchestra played and the atmosphere was especially joyous. I came there with a friend; I always loved to dance.

While on the dance floor, I saw from a distance a young girl sitting with her parents. In Europe, it was not the custom to allow girls aged 16-17 to go to parties and festivities alone. There was an immediate click between us and I asked her to dance. That evening we returned to the dance floor several times and spoke about meeting again.

Love at first sight.

Her name was Eva. From that evening until this day, our lives have been joined.

I finished basic training and on my first furlough, we met again.

Eva and I on The Beach

Eva lived with her family on Hasmonean Street in Tel Aviv. Like me, she was born in Czechoslovakia and immigrated to Israel in 1949 from her hometown of Bratislava. Eva and her family survived the Holocaust in the Novaky camp, a model labor camp built by the Germans for international display in order to show that Jews were working in reasonable conditions. In August 1944, there was a Slovak uprising in the camp: the gates were forced open and the Jews escaped. Eva was 11 years old and she had a younger brother. Both children were fair-haired and blue-eyed and Eva's parents found a local family to whom they paid a large sum to hide the children. Eva's parents hid in the nearby forest.

The family treated the two Jewish children well; there were many children in the villages and they assimilated among them. At a certain point, the money ran out and the children joined their parents in the forest. These were the winter days of 1944-1945. Eva's grandparents also hid with them in the woods, as did her mother's sister and her family.

Eva does not talk about this period in her life when the family wandered through the woods in the dead of winter, trying to reach liberated territory. Her grandparents did not make it and froze to death, which must have been extremely traumatic for the whole family.

Eva, her brother, and both parents finally reached an area controlled by partisan fighters and managed to survive. They returned to their hometown, Bratislava. There they found nothing that resembled the city they had left, and decided to immigrate to Israel. Eva's parents were used to living in a large, vibrant city, so they chose Tel Aviv. Their apartment at 5 Hasmonean Street was the main destination I came to on any vacation I received from the military.

Another moving encounter during my military service was meeting up with Yossi Greenwald, who was the quartermaster officer at my base. Yossi was the son of Rabbi Greenwald, who ran the last *heder* where I had studied before they deported us all to the ghetto. The Greenwald's home was next door to my cousins' house, and our meeting briefly gave me an inner journey into my childhood days.

The bond between Eva and me grew stronger. Most of the houses did not have telephones at the time, but luckily, Eva worked at a clothing store in Nahalat Binyamin Street. The shop had a telephone that allowed us to communicate and make plans.

After two and a half years, I completed my military service. Eva and I planned to get married immediately after I found a job and set myself up financially. On May 9, 1955, Lag B'Omer, we stood under the canopy in the same hall where we first met. The event was well attended, with many family members on both sides filling the hall.

It was one of the happiest days of my life.

In 1958, our eldest daughter, Orna, was born, followed in 1962 by her sister Anat.

Left: Our daughter Orna, our first-born
Right: Our two daughters, Orna and Anat

The birth of my daughters was exhilarating for me. I felt that my heart, which had been shrouded in layers of suffering and pain, opened to my little daughters. I have no words to describe how excited I was to become a father; I could nurture and care for them, and give them a real childhood in place of the one I had lost was so very important to me. We loved taking Orna and Anat on trips around the country and spent weekends and holidays in nature. I was happy.

Mom and Zev (Wilhelm) lived not far from us and every Friday Orna and Anat enjoyed staying at their house, so Eva and I were free to go out by ourselves and have fun.

Over the years, I have not talked about my experiences during the war. When I felt it was time to tell the girls a little about the suffering that had been our lot during the Holocaust, they stopped me.

"Dad, don't."

I think they did want to know, but were mature enough to listen only partially. I realized that to protect them it would be better to keep the past deep in my heart and memories. I did not want to grieve them and to convey to them the anguish that weighed upon our hearts then and is still with us to this day. Eva and I preferred not to impose on our daughters the burden of the recollection of all the infants, children, siblings, parents, spouses, and grandparents who were brutally murdered by the Nazis.

I believe that most Holocaust survivors kept silent for this reason. The desire was to protect the young souls of our families from going too deeply into what had happened to their parents. We preferred to take on ourselves the burden of memory of the years of terror rather than pass it on to our children. Thus, many Holocaust survivors began telling about the suffering they experienced during the Holocaust only when they were older, when the children were grown and were able to listen and understand. In addition, today we are encouraged to speak, but in those early years, young Israel was absorbed in a struggle for survival and was not able to provide a real setting for our survival stories.

In the 1970s, Shani, my friend and brother during the war and forever after, immigrated to Israel.

When I left Bergsas and crossed the border, Shani remained in the city. Although there was no one left of his family, he was in no hurry to leave and missed the opportunity before the borders were completely sealed.

In World War II, the interest of the Soviet Union and the United States was to defeat the common Nazi enemy, but after the war ended, breaches between the East and West widened and a period began known as the Cold War, in which the two powers battled each other for political control of the free world.

The vast areas liberated by the Soviet Union as it advanced westward in its war against Nazi Germany encompassed within its dominion what became known as the "Communist Bloc." The Soviets did much to establish communist rule in the areas they liberated/occupied and carried out population exchanges to ensure cooperation and loyalty.

Bergsas' population was now mostly Ukrainian and the city came to be called Beregovo. Czechoslovakia tried to claim that it was occupied territory, but the Soviet response was, "You lost the war - there is no going back." In the 1990s, when the Soviet Union collapsed and new nation states formed within its territory, the region officially became part of Ukraine.

When Shani came to apply for a passport, they asked for his name. "Joshua Itzkowitz," he replied. Remember, each of us had a Jewish name, in addition to a Czech name. As part of the process of deepening Soviet identity, it was imperative to stick to the local names. The militiamen looked at him and said, "There is no such name. From today, you are Alexander." That is how Shani became Alexander, with a wave of a hand. To this day, his official name in Israel is Alex.

After the Soviet consolidation of control and the closure of the borders to free movement, Shani/Alex realized that he was doomed to remain in the Soviet Union. When he reached enlistment age, he joined the Red Army and after his release, he married Marta, and studied cooperative management which helped him in the future to find a stable job in Israel as the financial manager of a shopping mall. He immigrated to Israel in the 1970s, when the first opportunity arose to emigrate from the Soviet Union.

Our reunion was very emotional. We had both lost our biological siblings, but the grim year we went through together connected us as brothers. Today, Shani lives in Kiryat Bialik. This year we will both be celebrating our 90th birthday.

In 1991, the Gulf War broke out. Eva's parents had great difficulty wearing the protective gas masks and to get them away from Tel Aviv, we traveled with them to a convalescence home on the Beit Aharon moshav, where we planned to stay until the troubles passed. My mother also joined us. During the sirens, we came together and spent the days in relative tranquility. After a few quiet days, we were told we could return home.

We arrived at our apartment in Ramat Gan. An inner feeling led me to move the sealed room we had prepared, to a more enclosed location in the apartment. At the end of that week, there was a warning siren. We were seated on the floor in the sealed room waiting, when a loud "boom" sounded near us. All the windows in the apartment shattered. Our house had been hit by powerful blast waves from a rocket that landed nearby. The front door split in two. The missile fell about 30 meters distance from us. Seven or eight private homes on the street were completely demolished. If we had been in the original glass-damaged sealed room, our fate would most likely have been different. In the room we were in, windows were shattered, but it was towards the back of the apartment and we were unharmed.

Israeli flags flew on all the balconies of the houses around us. The sight of the destruction reminded me of other days, but the Israeli flags flying in the wind were conclusive proof that these were completely different days.

The house was wrecked, and we had to move in with friends who came to us as soon as they heard about the missile falling on our street. We returned home only after the state had repaired our apartment.

A year later, in 1992, Mother passed away. She was 86 years old.

Mother's death has greatly affected the rest of my life. Along with her, I said goodbye to the last remnant of my nuclear family.

Gone was the thread connecting me to the home where I had grown up.

Unconsciously, I was looking for a way to keep the connection to my childhood home alive in my life as an adult as well.

I knew what it was that could preserve my connection to the family I grew up in, half of which I had lost in the Holocaust...

Jewish tradition.

As I have said, I came from a home that kept the traditions. Jewish customs and especially the observance of the Sabbath and holidays were part of my identity until we were expelled from our home. Like many Jews who survived the Holocaust, the atrocities I witnessed and things I experienced had undermined my faith. Eli Wiesel, who came from a very religious family, used to say that his faith went up in the smoke of the Auschwitz crematorium. Only at the age of 80, did he return to the bosom of Judaism and felt sorry for the many years when he had lost faith.

After the war, I felt no connection to Jewish tradition. To whom could I pray in light of what I had seen?

When I met Eva, I went back to the practice of some of the religious customs out of respect for her family, who were devout. In my heart, I lacked a genuine connection to the Jewish religion and its symbols.

However, my mother's death touched the heartstrings of my family's history.

I realized that the only way I could preserve the memory of my childhood home - my father and brother, and now my mother as well - was to keep alive the embers in whose light I had initially grown up. I went back to praying in the mornings, going to synagogue on Saturdays and holidays, and believing in the importance of keeping the commandments.

I felt I was coming home.

I realized that the way we grow up as children is deeply etched into the human psyche. Our values are at the heart of the education we receive.

Now that I was the last survivor from my parents' home, I knew I had to preserve the memory of the warm and loving Jewish home that was stolen from me at an early stage of my life.

In 1994, Steven Spielberg, the director of the film "Schindler's List" established the "Survivors of the Shoah Visual History Foundation." I first revealed my complete story in a three-hour video documentary. I felt that I was strong enough to recall the horrendous memories, in order to preserve them for future generations.

In the April 1995, the fifty-year jubilee of the end of the war and the liberation of Buchenwald, an emotional gathering was held at the Press House in Tel Aviv. Rabbi Israel Lau and Eli Wiesel, the most famous Jewish survivors of Buchenwald, spoke at that meeting. I remember Rabbi Lau's words: "We are all 50 years old" and added, "we were reborn on April 11, 1945."

Our family continued to grow. Our daughters got married and started their own families.

Orna had two sons - Itai and Ido, and Anat had a daughter and a son - Maya and Roy.

The birth of my grandchildren was a significant sign that our lives continued in a normal, happy way. The relationship with my grandchildren is close and meaningful for me. The children flood us with love and warmth, as only children know how to do. We saw them often and were there for them as they grew up.

Their happy childhood healed my soul.

Orna lives in Ramat Gan, not far from us, and we would see the grandchildren regularly.

Anat established her home in Moshav Nir Zvi. On Mondays, when the children were small, we would pick them up in the afternoons from the kindergartens and then the schools, prepare a hot meal for them, and enjoy watching them run around in the green surroundings, carefree.

I felt that I had managed to rise from the ashes and build a new life. In the course of the years, I received a certificate of appreciation from the municipality of Ramat Gan for rehabilitating my life. The past is present in my mind, but I believe that I have been able to separate it from everyday life and give my family a full, happy life.

The observance of the bar and bat mitzvahs of the grand-children evoked all the comparisons to my own childhood.

In the course of daily life, we do at every moment compare it to our past lives, but at special events like the bar mitzvahs, I took care of every detail to create a ceremony to give them a deeper understanding of Judaism's survival and connection to the past. It was very important for me to preserve the con-tinuation of the tradition of my parents' house.

It was at this point when the desire arose in me to docu-ment my story.

A Summary

The initiative to write my life story began with Dr. Limor Regev, a friend of my daughter Anat, with the aim of detailing a historical record for the benefit of future generations.

Over the years, my willingness to speak has become an inner need, along with a strong desire to tell my story to as many teenagers as possible and try to make them understand that I, too, like them was once a child...

And then, that child was no more...

When I was their age, my life turned upside down.

Now, from the perspective of my advanced age, it is difficult even for me to comprehend what I went through during the Holocaust, but the fact is, I am here.

I rose from the ashes like all the survivors of the camps.

We started families and chose life.

The key to understanding our capacity to recover lies in our contribution to the establishment of a state and a home for the refugee Jewish people.

The mechanism of emotional repression, which I developed the moment I said goodbye to my mother and Arnold in Birkenau, kept me going later in life, after the war. I believe that it would have been impossible for me to move on and live a happy life without storing the past as deep as possible in the depths of my heart.

There is no doubt that despite my efforts to rebuild my life after the war, I came to Israel emotionally wounded.

My body recovered, but the scars on my soul were still bleeding. Coming to Israel brought me comfort but the real emotional rehabilitation of my life was my service in the Israel Defense Forces. Conscription into an army that is mine, in a country that is mine healed my soul. Before that, I had to repeat to myself that there was nothing more to fear. When I held a weapon, I felt release, because this is my country. From now on, no one will be able to cast me out. Here we have an army whose purpose is to protect me. We have a Jewish state and as the children say, if anyone threatens me - I can fight back.

Many times during my military service when I was in charge of distributing light and heavy weapons, the image of a German soldier, holding a weapon pointed at me, came to my mind. If only we had weapons then, they would not have been able to lead one third of the Jewish people to extermination.

Even today, 75 years after the end of World War II, the Jewish people have not attained the population they had on the eve of World War II, in September 1939. The German government believed that most peoples of Europe, with some exceptions, would be happy to help in the extermination process. In my first testimony as part of the project established by American director Steven Spielberg, I said, "I point an accusing finger at all the nations of the world who did nothing to save Jews. Some even tacitly approved of the perpetrators of Hitler's final solution to eradicate Judaism." I am proud to say that the Czechs were among the exceptional peoples who did their best to help the Jews.

In Prague, near the Golem Synagogue, there is a building with a large sign in English and Hebrew, thanking the Czech people for their help in rescuing Jews.

I know that the ability to let go of the past and those we have lost, and to find happiness in life, is not something that can be taken for granted.

Many Holocaust survivors were unable to recover from the enormity of the loss they had sustained. They suffered from uncontrollable outbursts of anger at various times, and lived in the shadow of the past, which continued to haunt them.

One of the moments when I realized that the past would always be a part of me was on one of my trips with Eva to Austria. We stayed in a local Bed &Breakfast and when we left, I asked for the phone number so we could return in the future. The owner of the B&B read out the number tattooed on my arm, from my time as a prisoner in Buchenwald...

Although my mind has recovered, one wound remains open: the forced, quick and cruel parting from my childhood and my innocence. From the warmth of Mother's protective embrace on the pier in Birkenau, I was thrust into an altered, adult reality. It was almost impossible to preserve the belief I had held as a child, in God, in the world, and in humankind. Over the years since the war, I have had to call on strong mental reserves to deal with the deep sense of deprivation of having my childhood stolen from me.

Every time Orna or Anat ran to me and hugged me lovingly, I would remember that once, before the war, I was a child like that - a boy whose safe haven was in the embrace of his parents.

I can imagine how painful it was for my mother to lose the child within me at age 14. If I could go back, perhaps I would show her more how hard it was for me without her. I would let her feel that deep inside, despite everything, I was still the same child who parted from her that day, there on the platform.

Mother has passed away and it is too late to tell her all this... I return to her in the only way that came to my mind, through the religious tradition with which I was nurtured in my parents' home.

In this way, I have a grip on my childhood, my parents, and the world I have lost.

The first time I had to return to Bar Mitzvah customs was when I had grandchildren. From a young age, I promised the three boys that I would accompany them and prepare them for their bar mitzvah, and when the time came, I kept my promise.

I prepared the boys for their Haftarah studies and bought for them all they needed to continue the Jewish and family tradition. My physical journey with them brought with it a mixture of intense excitement and deep pain. Already at the bar mitzvah of my grandson Itai, which took place in Anat's garden at Nir Zvi, - as I blessed him, the memories floated up. Without willing it so, I compared it to my own bar mitzvah. I watched my eldest grandson and was thankful to see him loved and protected, surrounded by family and friends. I felt great pride at that moment.

At the bar mitzvah celebration of my youngest grandson, Roy, in Tel Aviv, the memories enveloped me again when I blessed him. I visualized at that moment how at my Bar Mitzvah I had stood alone in the synagogue, my father having been drafted into the labor battalions of the Hungarian army.

The feeling of missing out on my childhood will accompany me until the day I die. I recall the days of innocence that were stolen from me, when in a single moment I lost my home, was separated from my parents and little brother. I had to survive alone in a cruel world full of physical and emotional pain, knowing nothing of what happened to them

Something inside me will always miss those of my family members who did not survive the war, and especially my father and little brother.

In many ways, I have recovered, and in others, my soul remains wounded. I am unable to visit my hometown, even today. My relatives, the grandchildren of Fanny and Herman Marmelstein, traveled to Berehove/Bergsas about a year ago, and visited the site of my parents' house. When they returned, they said that a school now stands in our compound. At their grandparents' home in the Ardo suburb, they found the house where we played bowls as I recall.

I was excited by the story, but I have no desire to go here. I remember the feeling of alienation that came over me as I wandered the city streets after returning from the camps. I remember the contempt in the eyes of the neighbors, and their disappointment that we had survived and returned to the city.

When I think about it, there are two places I would like to go back to if I had the chance.

The first place I would be happy to return to is Dobřenice, the village where I spent my vacations as a child. That place holds only good memories for me: of a carefree childhood, the smell of the forest, the serenity of nature, the rippling of the waters of the spring, the fruit trees, children running around, and a loving hug from grandparents.

The second place I wanted to get to was Buchenwald, where I was freed, hungry and weak.

It was there I saw how the good in man defeats the evil, and how one person's courage can affect the fate of hundreds of children.

Instead of the sign at the camp gate, which symbolized the Germans' attempt to make us lose the solidarity and unity of man - I wanted to put a completely different message, a new sign.

I will inscribe on it: "We won."

Where the Germans chose to place the inscription "Every man to his own fate," one of the greatest rescue operations of the war took place. Humanity and compassion overcame evil.

I choose to conclude this story of my life with a message to the people of Israel and the State of Israel.

For 2000 years, we wandered and were persecuted. One-third of our people was annihilated.

We, the remnants of the Holocaust, believe it is time for greater unity among us, despite our differences in political viewpoints, because we are desirous of choosing life. I believe that our future will rise and fall on this.

Most important for me is that young people understand this message.

Unity is the basis of our continued existence and the foundation of our future.

It is the most significant motif for the future of the State of Israel.

Summary – Limor Regev

The first time I met Moshe was at the Bar Mitzvah of Roy, his grandson and the best friend of my son, Omer.

It was impossible not to be impressed by this man.

His eyes twinkled with the light of life, and the years were etched into his face in a smiling brightness that glowed from within. I could see the strength that had helped him survive, and I wanted to hear his story from his own lips.

At that moment, when Moshe blessed his grandson and gave him the books that had survived the Holocaust, I decided to document Moshe's story and approached my friend Anat, Moshe's daughter and Roy's mother. Moshe gave his consent and we set off.

The subject of the Holocaust has been close to my heart since I was a little girl.

My grandparents on both sides fled Poland and immigrated to Israel in Zionist youth movements a few years before the German occupation. Almost their entire extended family perished in the crematoria of Treblinka. I remember my grandfather Yaakov's frail voice, reeling off the names of his parents and seven brothers and sisters who were murdered in the Holocaust. On my literary journey with Moshe, I was accompanied by many faceless members of my family who were murdered in the extermination camps.

It is difficult to sum up the strength of Moshe's character and the privilege given me to accompany him on the paths of remembrance. Through his eyes, we discover a rich world of Jewish culture, which has disappeared forever.

Most importantly, this is the story of a child forced to grow up unwillingly - an ordinary, anonymous boy, looking forward to his bar mitzvah celebration, which was never to be.

The world he knew collapsed before his eyes. He had to fight every day for his inherent right to exist against all odds.

In Moshe's survival story, his unique character stands out, with qualities that helped him make courageous, intuitive decisions that sustained his body, and no less importantly, his soul.

The great pain of the loss of his childhood innocence, and the happiness that were cruelly torn from him are still present within him today, but they do not control him. His younger brother, father and an entire world that was destroyed did not prevent him from being able to feel and do all he could to recover from the trauma he went through. Today, in his 90's, Moshe swims three times a week and his physical strength is in line with his soul.

He maintains a lifestyle full of energy, with an inexhaustible thirst to experience and communicate with others.

Moshe's greatest triumph is his capacity to remain optimistic, to believe in the good in humankind, and to bring forth from the ashes a loving, stable and warm family for his daughters, grandsons and granddaughter.

At a get-together we had at Moshe's friend Shani's house, I looked at them and felt the intensity of the connection between the two of them: the shared excitement to meet, the concern for each other, the sorrowful eyes and distant gaze when the memories flood in, the tears that fall even now, seventy-five years after a slice of bread was stolen from them...

Two elderly men who in some ways have forever remained thirteen and a half years old.

I truly hope that the administration of "Yad Vashem" will grant Moshe the respect he deserves to light a flame at the state ceremony, which takes place every year on the eve of Holocaust Remembrance Day.

It was a great honor for me to document Moshe's story for the benefit of future generations.

This book is meant primarily for today's young people. It is important to Moshe that his life story can be for them a lesson in resourcefulness, courage, friendship, values and most importantly – a love of the land and a love for human-kind, so long as they are human...

Appendix -

Summary of the experiences of Moshe's family members during the war and after it ended:

The Kessler family, Moshe's father

Grandfather - Meir (Morton) - died of an illness in 1943
Grandmother - Clara – Auschwitz
Father - Herman - Killed by a stray bullet on the last day of the war
Mother - Paula - survived and immigrated to Israel
Brother - Arnold (8) - Auschwitz

<u>Uncles on my father's side, who lived together in the same compound</u>

Shlomo Leisinder - Auschwitz
Hannah (Hani) Leisinder – Father's Sister – Auschwitz
Magda Leisinder (14) Auschwitz
Zalman (Zulik) Leisinder) 10 (Auschwitz

<u>Uncles on the father's side – Berehove</u>

Isidore Kessler (father's brother) - survived the labor battalions, immigrated to the United States.
Rosa (Rosie) Kessler - Deported to Auschwitz and from there to Ravensbruck with my mother, survived and immigrated to the United States
Tibi Kessler - Auschwitz
Judith Kessler - Auschwitz
Meir Kessler - Auschwitz
Harold Kessler - born after the war - lives in the USA.

<u>Uncles on father's side – in Berehove – business partners</u>

Ignaz (Yitzhak) Lazarovich - Auschwitz
Malka Lazarowitz (father's sister) - Auschwitz
Yuli Lazarowitz - Auschwitz
Bella Lazarowitz – Auschwitz
Moshe Lazarowitz – Survived, enlisted in labor battalions and then in the provisional Czech army
Ilona (Ilo) Lazarovich - Survived, the first relative Moshe met in Burgsas, married and immigrated to Israel, no children
Barry Lazarowitz - Auschwitz
Magda Lazarowitz (the youngest daughter, two or three years older than Moshe) - Survived

<u>Uncles on my father's side who lived in the suburb of Ardo - Fanny</u>

Mermelstein (father's sister) - Auschwitz

Herman Mermelstein – Fanny's husband – Auschwitz

Moshe Marmelstein – Immigrated to Israel before the war

Avraham Mermelstein (Moss) - Hungarian labor camp, survived and immigrated to Israel

Rachel Marmelstein - Immigrated to Israel before the war

Margit Marmelstein – Auschwitz

Relatives on the mother's side -

<u>Grandparents (mother's parents)</u>

Zeev Blubstein – Auschwitz

Rebecca Blubstein - Died before the war

<u>Mother's brothers and sisters:</u>

Haim Blauvstein - Left for Israel in 1938

Miriam - (Older sister) married to Zigmund - deported in 1942 to Kaminski Podolsk - perished in the shooting pits

Sarna (Sarah) - Deported in 1942 to Kaminski Podolsk, perished in the shooting pits

Jacob and Rosie were married, deported to Auschwitz and from there to Bergen Belsen. Both of them survived and immigrated to Israel in the 1970's

Helen - Deported to Auschwitz and from there to Bergen Belsen. Survived, immigrated to Israel in the 70's

Iren - A few years older than me. We would spend all our summer vacations together. Deported to Auschwitz and from there to Bergen-Belsen. Survived and immigrated to Israel in 1949 with her husband, Jacob Zaks.

In conclusion:

Moshe's father had four sisters (Hani Leisinder, Rosa, Malka Lazarovitz, Fanny Marmelstein) and one brother (Isidore Kessler.) Of the six, two survived, Isidore and Rosa. Hani, Malka and Fanny were murdered at Auschwitz. Herman, Moshe's father, was shot and killed on the last day of the war.

Moshe's mother had five sisters (Miriam, Sarna, Rosie, Helen, Iren) and two brothers (Chaim, Jacob.) Of the eight, five survived. Chaim immigrated to Israel before the war and the other four survived the war: Helen, Rosie, Iren and Paula (Moshe's mother). Two sisters, Miriam and Sarna, were murdered in the shooting pits in Poland. In 1942 Jacob was murdered at Auschwitz.

PHOTOGRAPHS

Family event in the 1930s. My grandparents are seated in the middle, second row from the front. Immediately in front of them are Arnold and me. My father is in the back row, second from left, my mother in front of him, with the large white collar. Shani is in the front row on the far left.

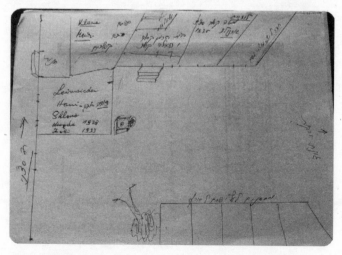

Sketch from my childhood home in Berehove

My mother Paula and sister Margot, 1911

Left: Iren, Mother, and Helen after the war
Right: My mother and Margot, 1938

15. 4 1987.

Letter I wrote to Eli Weisel, recalling the prayer at Buchenwald on the eve of Pesach

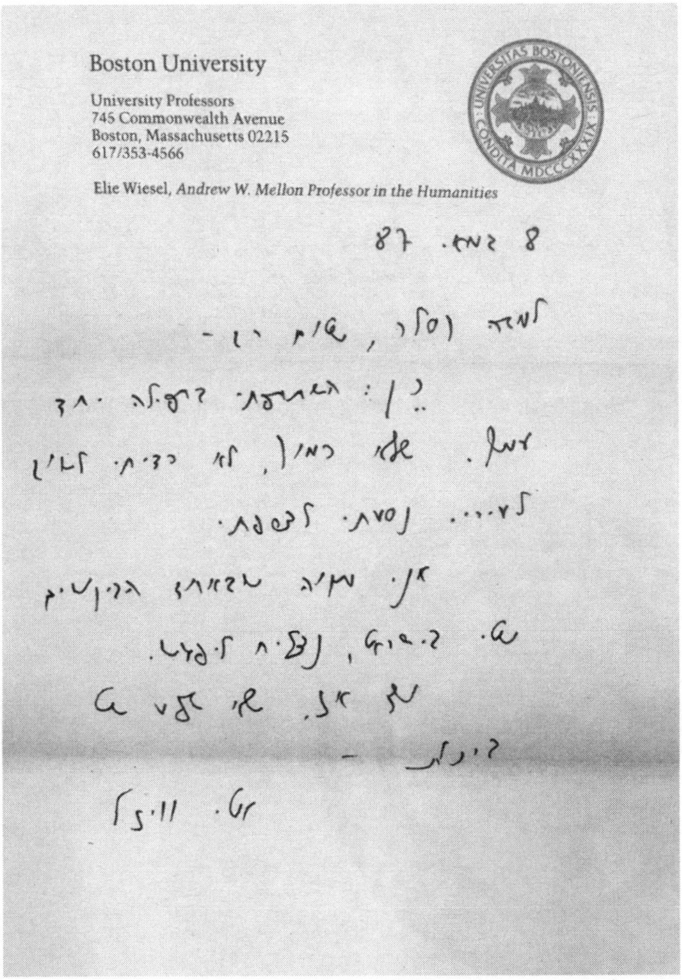

Boston University

University Professors
745 Commonwealth Avenue
Boston, Massachusetts 02215
617/353-4566

Elie Wiesel, *Andrew W. Mellon Professor in the Humanities*

8 במרץ 87

למור נסלר, שלום רב –

כן: המשפחה [illegible] אחד
[illegible]. שלא כמוני, לא ראיתי [illegible]
לצערי... נספתה בשואה.
אני שמח [illegible] [illegible]
[illegible], [illegible] [illegible].
[illegible]
בברכה –
אלי ויזל

Eli Weisel's reply to my letter

Hungarian ID issued during my journey home in 1945.

Moshe Kessler and Shani Itzcovitz 2020

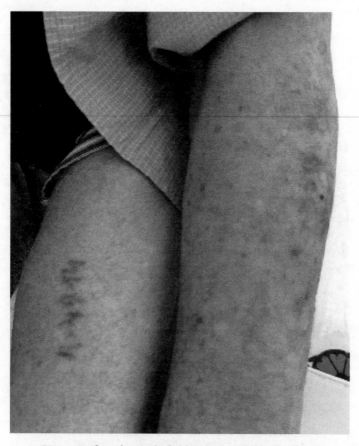

75 years after the end of the war, we still bear the ID numbers the Germans tattooed on our forearms. Two teenagers with two numbers that have joined us in a bond forever. A-4913 / A-4914

VICTORY

Moshe and Limor 2021

Postcript

The Boy From Block 66 was given to Moshe Kessler for his ninetieth birthday in September 2020. We had printed only fifty copies.

It is not an easy task to put into words the life and soul of a man who went through hell, and I hoped that Moshe would be pleased with the result. The first time he read the book, he was moved to tears and said that it had felt like watching a movie about his life.

Two months after Moshe's ninetieth birthday, in November 2020, his best friend and brother in the terrible suffering of the Holocaust, Shani, passed away. He was ninety years old. COVID-19 was at its peak and no vaccine had yet been developed, so restrictions and lockdown prevented Moshe from attending his closest friend's funeral. He was heartbroken.

Moshe and Shani had kept in touch over the years and six months earlier, in March 2020, Moshe and I travelled together to visit Shani as part of our research for the book. I photographed them both, and their pictures are featured in the book. We did not know then that that was the last time they would meet and the last photograph that would ever be taken of them together.

In January 2021, only two months after Shani's death, Moshe's wife Eva passed away, too. Eva and Moshe had spent seventy long years together.

Within three months, Moshe had lost Shani, who had been a brother to him since the age of thirteen, and Eva – the love of his life.

Despite the unbearable dual loss he had suffered, Moshe was able to muster incredible strength of spirit to keep on living, and to continue to tell his story for the sake of future generations.

In May 2021, the book was launched festively in the presence of his friends and family, who were adamant that it was too good to be limited to such a small group of people.

Following excellent reviews, I decided to turn Moshe's story into a legacy that would last for generations, so I submitted the story to a publishing house that translated it into English and published it on Amazon. Moshe and I were overwhelmed as we saw the book become a bestseller and go on to be translated into five additional languages: Czech, Italian, Spanish, Russian, and Albanian.

After the war, Moshe refused to visit his home city of Berehove, Auschwitz, or any other place that reminded him of that terrible time in his life.

In April 2022, in memory of his dear friend and in light of the book's success, Moshe decided to return to Buchenwald for the first time since the liberation of the camp. He and

Shani had always discussed returning to the camp someday as victors, but only Moshe was able to return.

The fourteen-and-a-half-year-old boy who exited through the camp's gates in April 1945 entered them again at the age of ninety-one, accompanied by his warm and loving family and supported by two of his grandchildren. I was there with them and so was the main Israeli TV news channel, to document this moving moment.

Moshe gave the Buchenwald archive a photograph of him and Shani and shared with me that it was as though he was there for both of them.

After writing the book and learning about the incredible story of the children of Block 66, I was compelled to go to the Czech Republic and visit the family members of Antonin Kalina, the children's saviour. I met with his niece and two of his nephews who had known him well and were happy to talk about him.

I realised then that the world should know about this wonderful person, who was a powerful ray of light in a world of darkness, and so I set out on another journey of writing.

Antonin Kalina's life story will be published in 2024.

Today, Moshe is almost ninety-three years old. He swims twice weekly and makes an effort to stay in shape. After years of silence, he now shares his story regularly. The process of writing the book sparked his desire to share his history with the world.

I have had the utmost privilege to partake in the journey of this amazing and inspiring man, the boy from Block 66.

Limor Regev, June 2023

Moshe Kessler and his family,
walking away from Buchenwald camp.